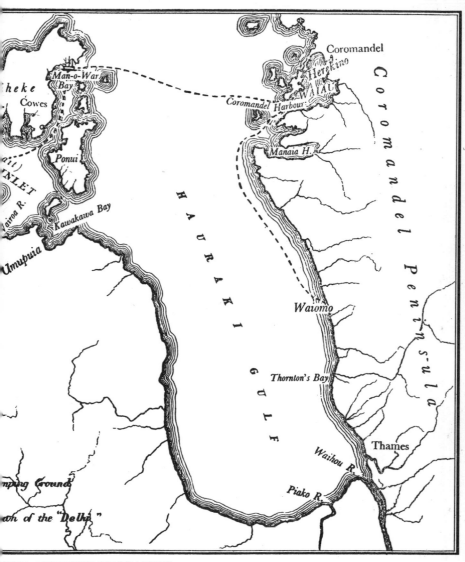

THE AUTHOR'S NARRATIVE

ng in the 1898 issue of *Poenamo*

POENAMO

NEW ZEALAND CLASSICS

POENAMO
JOHN LOGAN CAMPBELL

Golden Press
in association with Whitcombe & Tombs Limited

First published 1881
This edition published 1973
by Golden Press Pty Ltd
16 Copsey Place
Avondale, Auckland
and
35 Osborne Street
Christchurch
Printed in Hong Kong
ISBN 0 85558 277 4

Contents

BOOK FOURTH

How a New Colony is Born to an Old Nation

Introduction

By JOAN STEVENS

POENAMO, published anonymously in London in 1881, is the work of Dr (afterwards Sir) John Logan Campbell, 'the Father of Auckland', and gives a first-hand account of Maori life and Pakeha settlement in the Hauraki and the Waitemata in 1840-41. Campbell speaks of it as 'a plain unvarnished tale', but it is certainly not this, except in the sense of being the truth. Campbell is no horny-handed amateur struggling with a pen, as have been so many authors of pioneer memoirs, but a skilled writer with a fascinating story to tell. To the interest of his matter is added the attractiveness of his manner, with the result that *Poenamo* is one of the best of its class. It is little known only because copies of the book have been scarce.

John Logan, born 3 November 1817 in Edinburgh, was the only surviving son of Dr John Campbell, of the family of Aberuchill and Kilbryde. He took his medical degree in 1839 and sailed for Australia in the *Palmyra* in July of that year. At Adelaide, William Brown, a Dundee lawyer, and his wife, joined the ship and made friends with the young surgeon. They parted at Sydney, Brown to cross to the Bay of Islands to see what New Zealand could offer, while Campbell looked at Australia. Not liking the prospects, he left for Wellington in the *Lady Lilford* in March 1840. It seemed unlikely that he would meet Brown, but Mrs Brown gave him letters 'just in case'.

On arrival at Port Nicholson, Campbell and a Scots shipmate named McInnes camped 'at the mouth of the

small river Hutt' where the settlement then was. 'We lived
in the tent for a fortnight', wrote Campbell, 'explored the
valley of the Hutt, and to our minds found it wanting.'
They therefore shipped again on the *Lady Lilford* which
was going to the Hauraki Gulf.

On the morning of 13 April 1840 they sailed in to
Waiau (Coromandel), and dropped anchor off Herekino,
the trading station of Big Webster on Whanganui Island.
'On going ashore', says Campbell, 'who should greet me
but my *Palmyra* friend.' It certainly seemed as if fate was
determined to link the fortunes of Brown and Campbell.
Together with McInnes (Makiniki) and Cook, they
formed the 'Scotch quartet' who explored the Waitemata
with Webster in early May 1840, and who, but for a 'mess
of pottage', as *Poenamo* relates, might have bought the
site of Auckland. Brown and Campbell are the 'we ither
twa'' and the 'Senior and Junior partners' of the book.
Brown was then 32 years old.

After the failure of their attempt to buy on the mainland, the partners bought the little island of Motu-Korea.
Its owners, the Ngati Tamatera, lived down the Gulf at
Waiomu, and with them and the Pakeha sawyer James
Palmer (Pama), the two men spent three months, hewing
out a kauri canoe and gaining an insight into Maori ways
of life.

On 13 August 1840 they at last crossed to their island,
and, after buying pigs from Kawau of the Ngati Whatua
at Onehunga, built a raupo whare and began their farming
venture. Captain Hobson, they discovered, had likewise
explored the Waitemata during the winter, and had
selected a site there for the New Zealand capital. Thus
Campbell's dream came true. The official party arrived on
16 September 1840 to found the city of Auckland.

On 21 December, Brown and Campbell established 'the
Firm' by pitching the tent at Commercial Bay, in the new
settlement—'a stone's throw from the beach where stood
the Government store .... the tide then washed a
gravelly beach where now stands the Post Office—the

beach ended in a small tidal creek . . . . a noble pohutukawa stood sentinel. . . .' In Campbell's manuscript of
his reminiscences, this description is accompanied by a
photograph of a sketch, probably one commissioned to
send home to his parents as was his habit. (See page 32.)
He cut his firewood, he notes, 'on the mound whereon
stands the Wesleyan chapel'.

At the sale of town lots in April 1841, 'the Firm' bought
land in Shortland Street, and erected at the back of the
block near O'Connell Street the kauri dwelling 'Acacia
Cottage' which is now preserved in Cornwall Park.
Business prospered. In 1844 Brown went to England, finding time on the five months' voyage to write *New Zealand
and its Aborigines,* of which the first two chapters, written
in 1840, cover the same experiences at Waiomu as those
described in *Poenamo.*

Campbell's knowledge of the Maori people proved
valuable. He became a great friend of Maning of Hoki-
anga, with whom he visited Waka Nene's war camp in
April 1845. Maning is the authority for his anecdote of
the missionary and heathen priests at their incantations.

In 1848 Campbell left for a long visit to the Continent
and his Scottish home, returning in 1851 only to set off at
once for a trip to California. 'The Firm' continued to grow.
Its owners played a major part in the affairs of the colony.
Brown held high political office, and established the
Southern Cross (later amalgamated with the *New Zealand
Herald*). Campbell founded the Auckland Savings Bank,
organized the first Volunteer Rifle Corps, and in 1855
became Superintendent of the Province of Auckland. In
1853 he bought land at Maungakiekie (One Tree Hill);
most of this is now Cornwall Park, which he presented
to the people of Auckland in 1901.

Campbell often refers to his wanderlust, and confesses
to his children that he was 'a terrible peregrinator'. The
years 1856-70 were spent travelling, mostly in Europe. In
1858 he married Emma Wilson, daughter of John Cracroft
Wilson, then judge of Mooradabad, India, and later well

known in public life in Canterbury. There were four children, for two of whom *Poenamo* was written—Ida, born 1858, and Winifred, born 1864. A baby died during their Auckland visit of 1861-2, and the only son, three-year-old Logan, in Florence in 1867. Frightened by this disaster and by Ida's white cheeks, the Campbells settled in Scotland for 1867-8. It was here, 'at Deeside . . . . sitting by the river near the Invercauld Arms', that Campbell began to compose his scattered journal and letter material into memoirs which should make clear to his 'two darlings' their family history and their father's doings. The decision to return to New Zealand had already been taken, and he wished to give his children some understanding of the land which was really their home.

The manuscript volume that resulted, *Reminiscences,* is now in the Library of the Auckland Museum. It is a stout wooden-bound quarto book with a large lock. The pages are covered with neat level writing, and with inserted photographs, letters, sketches, cuttings, etc., of all kinds. Of this manuscript, the first 297 pages, about half the total, are embodied in *Poenamo,* and bring the story down to early 1841. The remainder has not been printed. It completes the record of Campbell's personal and public life to the date of the family's return to Auckland in 1870. 'And having brought you to that home on the lovely Waitemata's shore', ends Campbell, 'I must leave it to yourselves to chronicle all the changes'—how they planned a new home, 'Kilbryde', and how in his latter days as in his first 'old Papa' would look out over the water to Motu-Korea and the Coromandel ranges.

There is a postscript, dated Kilbryde 1883. This describes Ida's death abroad in October 1880. (The girls were sent home for their education in 1876.) *Poenamo* was then ready for the printer and was published early in 1881. Campbell did not alter its references to 'my children'. He records sadly 'and now only one remained to me to read it.' Mrs Winifred Humphreys (Campbell) is now living in London—there are no grandchildren.

Introduction

In 1907, Campbell compiled a further memoir entitled 'My Autobiography. A Short Sketch of a Long Life 1817-190-? by the author of *Poenamo*'. This manuscript covers briefly the same ground as *Poenamo* and the *Reminiscences*, with fuller treatment of his student days, and with details of his family affairs and Auckland interests from 1870. He also tried his hand at imaginative literature, writing short stories, and 'Trespiano, a Tale of Florence' (not published), written on shipboard in 1880.

Dr. Campbell was knighted in 1902 in recognition of his services to the city. The list of his activities is too long to repeat, but includes wide business, political, and cultural interests, as well as generous support of many worthy causes. He died on 22 June 1912, and was buried on the summit of Maungakiekie.

Poenamo, the published first half of the *Reminiscences*, is a book of very mixed origin. The core of it was written when Campbell was thirty-three. Like Brown, he made good use of a long sea voyage. 'I spent my time' he says of his return on the *Royal Saxon* in 1850, 'in writing up the rough sheets of my Motu-Korea manuscript.' And again, on the *Helen Page* from California in 1851, 'I finished my Motu-Korea manuscript—the captain having a good cry over one of the chapters.' This 'Motu-Korea manuscript' covers books 2, 3, 4, of *Poenamo*. Campbell worked from his own journals, and from letters sent home and gathered again by him during his 1848-50 visit. His sister Kate versified for him at that time his translation of the dirge chanted over Ngatai. Possibly the chapter on the death of his sister Regina (omitted in this edition) was also written at this date. It is difficult to see what else in 'my Motu-Korea manuscript' a tough sea-captain could have cried over.

At Deeside in 1867-8, Campbell inserted some connecting remarks addressed to his children, and wrote for them an introduction relating his pedigree and boyhood, voyage to Australia, and meeting with the Browns.

In this state the *Reminiscences* remained till 1875, when

according to his own note Campbell added the chapters dealing with 1841-70. Little of this 1875 material appears in *Poenamo*, except some details about early Auckland, such as the episode of the drunkard, and the picture of 'our first Magistrate Mr Dawson' dispensing justice under the canopy of heaven. Some fatherly philosophizings at the end also belong to 1875.

Finally, in 1877-80 Campbell revised the first thirty-one chapters for the press, and invented the melodious but incorrect Maori title, *Poenamo*. This is his version of *pounamu* (greenstone), which appears in the Maori name for the South Island, Te Wai Pounamu ('Water of Greenstone').

This press revision of 1880 involved some tidying up of style, suppression of names, omissions and corrections of detail. More important is Campbell's addition of an over-riding commentary, born of the nostalgia with which he recalled 'that long long ago morning forty years since', when he was young and 'verdi', and the Waitemata lay before him. This gives the book perspective, a to-and-fro movement in time, a characteristic personal flavour, and unity of theme. The freshness of immediate experience is retained, for it is no 'old Papa' who writes of the timber-draggers, and bargaining for pigs, and the Maori philosophy of *taihoa* (by-and-by). But we have also the mellow haze which even 'half a memory' will provide for a pioneer looking back. The mixture is attractive and unusual. The faults of the book are partly those of the day, sentimentality, and some heavy verbal antics—and partly those of its haphazard origin. It is after all a private family document. Its merits may be left to speak for themselves. The combination of unique subject-matter, breadth of treatment, and literary skill is rare enough in early New Zealand writing to make the book remarkable. It is entitled, equally with Maning's *Old New Zealand,* to be one of our classics.

The following details will serve to round off the picture given in *Poenamo*.

Introduction

William Webster (Wepiha) was the most important trader in the Hauraki in the eighteen-thirties, and made history later with his claim to have bought 500,000 acres of land. Litigation over this claim, several times revived, and dealt with at the highest international level, ran its course from 1840 to 1925.

Herekino, Webster's trading station, was in a sheltered little bay on the inner side of Whanganui Island, Coromandel Harbour. The island, known locally as Purser's or Mannion's Island, is separated from a long finger of mainland by a narrow tideway called 'Little Passage', which Campbell mentions.

Waiomu is on the Hauraki coast just north of Thames, and is now a popular camping beach. A huge isolated rock, crowned by a pohutukawa tree, is traditionally 'Campbell's rock'. He is said to have pitched his tent in its shelter, and the stream still runs nearby.

Motu-Korea (Brown's Island) lies off the entry to the Tamaki River. Its present owners are the Auckland Metropolitan Drainage Board, who propose to set up there a modern plant for treatment of the City sewage. Alas for Campbell's 'little sea-girt possession.' The name Motu-Korea means, according to a note by James Cowan, 'island of the pied oyster catcher', a seabird once numerous in the Gulf. It was famous in Maori days for the kumera and taro crops grown in its volcanic soil. Owing to the Government's proclamation controlling transfer of land, Brown and Campbell were uneasy about their purchase, in spite of the good offices of Captain Symonds, the Deputy, and were indeed nearly dispossessed by Hobson, who wanted to farm the island himself. But *taihoa* won the day once more, and Hobson died before anything was done. The island pig-station was not without its troubles, however, for 'the Firm's' pigs were spirited away by a rascally ex-convict, Abraham. This is the episode of the Pakeha thieves to which Campbell refers. To his bitter regret, Campbell sold Motu-Korea. 'I would sacrifice much', he wrote in 1907, 'to be able to call it my own again. . . . I look with longing eyes away upon the little crater summit.'

James Cowan has the following note on the 'mess of pottage' incident:

'Apihai te Kawau, the patriarchal head chief of the Ngati Whatua who sold the site of Auckland to the Government, is frequently mentioned by Campbell. Te Hira, the young chief who figures in the pigeon-stew story of Orakei and who, in his fit of sulks, baulked the first land-buying expedition of the Waiau party, was Te Kawau's son. I remember Te Hira as he was in his old age; I saw him at Orakei village several times before his death in 1888. He and that fine old friend of the Pakeha, Paora Tuhaere, were the principal chiefs of Ngati Whatua. Both were tattooed of face; Paora wore the side-whiskers of John Bull; Te Hira was an aristocratic looking, white-moustached ancient. They were the last surviving relics of the olden time, the period which the pages of *Poenamo* so entrancingly preserve for us.'

JOAN STEVENS

Victoria University College
June 1952

Bibliography

1881 *Poenamo. Sketches of the early days in New Zealand. Romance and reality of Antipodean life in the infancy of a new colony.* Williams and Norgate, London, 1881 (anonymous) [some copies with a map].

1898 *Poenamo.* Re-issue, with illustrations by Kennett Watkins, 1888, new map and half-title. Upton and Co., Auckland. [150 copies of the 1881 edition in loose sheets were sent out to Campbell, who had illustrations prepared in 1888 by Kennett Watkins. When the illustrated issue was finally made in 1898, map and half-title were copied and bound up with the title page and sheets of 1881.]

In this 1952 edition of *Poenamo,* to enable the modern reader to come quickly to the author's narrative of his colonial experiences, the first four chapters of the original edition have been reduced to one. This abridgement has been achieved, it is hoped, without deleting any material fact in the author's story of his early life. Apart from this the text is complete from Chapter V of the original edition (now Chapter II), which begins with the departure from Scotland. It should be noted, however, that although Miss Joan Stevens has provided the introduction to this edition of *Poenamo* she has not been responsible for editing the text. The new edition was planned for publication before 1940, and the work of normalizing the author's often unusual spelling of Maori words, and of interpreting them, was done by the late James Cowan, whose footnotes are distinguished from the author's by being placed within square brackets.

BOOK FIRST

Myself

CHAPTER I

Why and How I became a Doctor : Decision to Emigrate

I WAS an only son. If my father had only been the same, he would have succeeded to the title and estate of our family. But not having been imbued with the proper appreciation of the value of these in this world, he allowed himself to be born the youngest of the family, one of fourteen too, and with such a large proportion of brothers that for him to look forward to succeed to the title through such a vista of male heirs as kept cropping up in the shape of nephews, would have been as hopeless a task as trying to see to the end of the list of his own Scotch cousins!

My grandfather had married twice. The consequence was, that before my father saw the light the children of his eldest sister—step-sister—did so, and he had nephews and nieces who used to dandle their uncle on their knees. The hospitality of the old castle that had to be extended to the direct members of the family—not to mention 'Hielan' cousins and retainers—was enough to drain a heavier purse than the old gentleman's, so he got very handsomely indeed into debt, and, being an honest man, he foolishly sold off all the unentailed portion of the fine old family estate to make himself square with the world and his own conscience. And so it fell out that the old castle and the barony lands were all that were left, and, in fine, to tell a sad story in a few words, my grandfather

B

died having only as many hundreds a year as his father had thousands, and *sic transit gloria* of old families!

My dear worthy father's idea of starting in the world was after this fashion: he fell in love and married when he was only a boy of four-and-twenty. He began life with a wife and seven-and-sixpence a day as a surgeon in the Army, when the whole world was gazing with fear and wonder at that fiery meteor Napoleon the First, whose after-consignment to St. Helena disbanded my father's regiment and sent him afloat on the world with his young wife and two young children, and no seven-and-sixpence a day to help them!

I was not a bright boy; I was not a stupid one. Indeed, I have a kind of feeling now that I was one of those dreary, sensible boys who provoke people because they find a fellow is so sensible—for a boy. At school I did not shine, and could only just manage to keep a little above the middle of my class. I well remember I used to wonder why this was so, because I felt myself a better fellow than those beside me, and my companions were invariably those at the head of the class. In after-years the reason why dawned upon me, and I came to the conclusion—in confidence to myself—that I really should have been a tremendously clever man if I had not, most unfortunately for myself and the world at large, of course, been born with only— half a memory! This has been my bane through life; to save that life I could not at this moment tell you the year in which I was born.

My school-days were pain and grief to me. I learned, but only to forget; it was as hopeless as the task of trying to carry water in a sieve. I grew up a horrid, classic-less, sensible lad; I laboured at Latin and Greek through the accepted curriculum of school and college for over six years—in my case a direful waste of my young life. My masters thought well of me, over-much of me, though only figuring in the middle of my class; but I did differ from those on each side of me, for they never attempted an essay, and I always got my half-holiday for my composition.

And what next? What was I going to be? Of course I was going to be a doctor—it never entered my mind to be anything else—it was a fixed and determined thing before I had brains enough to think about it myself. And I found myself becoming a doctor accordingly.

But as the time kept slipping past which was converting me into a doctor, I had brains enough to force home the conclusion that when I fairly was one, the sticking up my name on a brass plate on the door, below my father's, with 'Junior' on it, would not add to his practice; nor did I see, as long as he was alive and well, how it would bring me any. And so it came about that by degrees, slow but sure, it became a fixed idea in my mind that I would push my fortune abroad somewhere or other.

Doubtless you will be wondering how it came about that a man with only half a memory managed to pass his examinations, but with superhuman perseverance I did so. True, I was still a mere sieve, but I kept pouring the thousands of facts which I had to be up in, in such an incessant stream through my brain that the necessary quantum got entangled therein somehow or other for the ordeal of examinations. But it was hard work.

My enterprising mother saw, and nobly joined me in saying, there would be no use in my remaining at home after taking my degree. The old gentleman did not take at all kindly to that idea: he would have been quite content to have seen the second brass plate with the 'Junior' on the door. Indeed, my mother and I had to canvass privately the friends through whose good offices there was a prospect of procuring a commission in the East India Company's service, for I had determined to enter upon that field of enterprise.

I well remember the one prominent and prevailing desire of my heart was, that some day I should see the world. I believe it was this feeling which was the moving spirit in determining me to have no second brass plate underneath my father's. I believe it was this feeling that

decided me to try for *the Company's* service. And I well
know the book that first kindled this deep desire: it was
Mungo Park's *Travels in Egypt*.

The end of winter still found me struggling hard to
narrow the meshes of my sieve-like memory and hold in
the *quantum sufficit* to face my examiners, but with the
spring came a new light as to my future, unlooked-for
prospects opened up, and it became a question whether
I should dare this new path or continue in the beaten
track I had chosen. I had no idea, however, of letting one
rope go before getting hold of another, so I carried my
midnight labours to a successful issue, and duly became
an M.D. and surgeon of the Edinburgh Schools of
Medicine.

But now rose another question: was I to follow the
profession I had chosen, or 'throw physic to the dogs'?
The new path which had opened up was one in the great
new world—not the Western, but the Great South Land
of Australia.

Was I to be, or not to be, a medical officer in *the Company's* service, and risk the climate of India, or become a
squatter in the plains of Australia, and make a fabulous
fortune by 'growing wool'? (I am now writing of the
years 1838-9, when the first great excitement prevailed
with regard to Australia, and when the first great stream
of emigration set out towards that colony.) The return
of some connections of my family, who had been early
settlers there, soon turned the scale, as far as I was concerned, in favour of my descending from the high estate
of M.D. to shepherd.

True, if I failed in that walk in life I could still fall
back upon my profession. But my being an M.D. could
do the sheep no possible harm, while I looked after them,
while possibly I might shoot with two strings to my bow,
and be a bush doctor as well

At last my dear cautious father got bitten with the
mania for Australia, and my mother, improving the
occasion, ended by talking him over to the new opening

for the only son. The old gentleman was only too glad to get rid of the East India Company's service, having a dread that the climate might bring his only son to an untimely end! So he dropped into the excitement of the day—the making a fortune in Australia.

And had I not much to learn before I left? Truly yes. My life hitherto had been purely a college one. I had, it is true, generally passed my summer vacations with relations in the country, where I had seen farming operations going on, in which I had helped in a very small way. I could load a cart with sheaves of corn, and take it to the stockyard. I could even build the stack—all save the top! I had seen bulls, and cows, and steers, and really knew one from the other quite well; but when I heard my country friends from Australia talking about ewes and maiden ewes, and wethers and hoggets, I felt I was *not* 'up in sheep' as an intending shepherd ought to be.

I laid my plans accordingly, and made a rush at the acquisition of some knowledge of the various trades which I hoped would serve me in good stead in my future life at the Antipodes. When my eight o'clock in the morning class at college ended with the winter session I exchanged the college for the carpenter's shop, and I used to commence there at seven.

My studies now were a strange mixture, as it was quite a question whether my professional or my trade knowledge was going to serve me best in after-life. Of course I took kindly to the carpenter's shop, for I had always displayed a strong mechanical bent, and was never happier than when at work at some carpentry or other. As my college education came to an end so did my apprenticeship at the carpenter's shop, but at the end of the spring session I had served three months at it, and had produced a huge splendidly dovetailed tool-chest, which was to carry an ample supply of tools for Antipodean use. It was carpentering at early morn, then a turn at college, then a rush between lectures to the cattle-market, and to where the cattle were slaughtered, or how else could I have known whether sheep were skinned and pigs scalded, or *vice versâ*—a most necessary knowledge when I had made up my mind to go to the uttermost parts of the earth, and very likely might have to do everything myself, or superintend others who knew no better! Then one required to know how to mend a saddle-girth, and to be able to do that one required to know how to put a bristle on the thread that had to be used. I found it so much more easy to remember all these things that I *saw,* than to remember the minute anatomy of the eye which saw them, which I had to remember by the aid of memory alone, that I found my day studies much more simple than my night ones.

But they all came to a conclusion in early summer. I had passed my examinations, and written a wonderful thesis (lying unappreciated in the archives of the University to this very day), proving how the tongue was not the organ of taste, thus complying with the last requirement before going through the ceremony of being 'dubbed'. But as this dubbing of neophytes was forbidden unless they were of the age of one-and-twenty, and as I had not as yet attained that ripe age of green manhood at the time of the last dubbing, and should not be forthcoming when the next one came off, the Senatus Academicus had to make a special case of it, and allow me to be dubbed by proxy, keeping back my parchment certificate of M.D. until after said dubbing ceremony, which came off in August, had been gone through.

But it was now only June. The time had come, however, that was to witness my departure from the parental roof. The only son was bidding it farewell, starting on his pilgrimage in life. The inheritance to which he was succeeding was simply that which he could carve out for himself in the race for life, the patrimony in hand summed up in his education of M.D. and a five-hundred-pound note! My worthy father had come to believe so completely in 'keeping sheep' in Australia that he had raised a thousand pounds, giving me one-half, the other to be invested by me on his account.

CHAPTER II

" Ho! for the Great South Land "

I SAILED from Greenock in July, 1839, in the good ship *Palmyra,* Brown master, bound for Adelaide, Melbourne, and Sydney, a new vessel starting on its first voyage.

Next to the captain I was the most important person on board—I was the doctor, not the officer of that name who rules over the ship's galley, and who really is of more importance on board a vessel than the veritable captain.

I was the medical officer in charge of the ship. It had been duly advertised in the newspapers—'carries an experienced surgeon . . . . and a cow'. If we were not actually coupled in the same sentence, we were in such close proximity that intending passengers by the vessel looked somehow on the one animal as of as much importance to them as the other. It is quite possible that the quadruped was in some eyes the more important.

To me, however, being coupled with the cow was not to be lightly thrown away. Indeed, I submitted to the conjunction for a valuable consideration in the shape of a saving of seventy guineas for my passage, and the additional comfort of a cabin to myself. It was a *very* small one truly, but still what a comfort!

The ship, only some 500 tons, was crowded: nearly fifty in the cabin, as many in the intermediate, and as many in the steerage, and the crew in addition.

I soon had my hands full: we had six days of our first start down Channel as rough as well might be, tacking, with double-reef topsails, with the wind dead ahead.

It was 'Where's the doctor?' every five minutes, and the poor doctor, just as sick as those who sent for him, was groaning with sea-sickness; but I had to jump up and go and write useless prescriptions for that vile ailment, and make them up myself as best I could.

I don't doubt I was set down as the very stupidest of doctors, and probably most of my patients thought the cow was worth half-a-dozen of me. I had so little time to think of my own sea-sickness, that I am sure I got over it all the sooner. But I had three days' very handsome benefit of that hideous infliction. Imagine having to get up with a splitting headache and go to the steamy steerage with all ports shut! I had to rush up again and gasp at the vessel's side, and then down again to another patient who had tried to seize me as I had rushed away from the last. But after three days I had fought the battle out with the enemy, vanquished him, and cast him out for evermore. Since those days I have made voyages in every conceivable kind of vessel, down to as small a one as would have gone inside the *Palmyra's* saloon, but I have never been sea-sick again. I have been sorely tried in small screws from Havre to the Thames, when I have been the only one who kept captain and sailors company in defying the enemy, but I have done it!

On the sixth night we had been out it was blowing and raining hard, a dead foul wind, and we were pitching into a heavy sea, when about midnight, just as I was struggling along the dark, slippery deck to my cabin from visiting a steerage passenger, I heard the boatswain sing out, 'My God! there's a ship bearing right down upon us that will cut us in two. Hard down there!' he yelled. I looked into the darkness and saw a great dark mass full sail close to us. On it came as if going right over us. It was rather too close a shave. The ship struck us, not in the hull, but the cutwater, carrying away the figure-head, breaking off our bowsprit as if it had been a carrot, and slowly ground past our bows with a sound through the gale as if merely breaking some matches. At that moment we did not know whether we had been struck in the hull or not, and the next yell that came from the boatswain was, 'Carpenter, sound the pumps'. It was a few moments of intense anxiety, but 'No water in the pumps', in the carpenter's voice, made us all breathe more freely. Then the next moment there rang through the ship from a dozen voices, 'Stand clear to leeward—the foremast is going by the board', and the next moment down came the stupendous mass, smashing the bulwarks to the deck just before the main rigging, carrying away maintopmast also. Fortunately we had all stood clear, and not a soul was hurt, so the surgeon's experience was not needed. I sat up to see all the wreck cut away and let go, for the great masts and yards were battering against the ship's side as if to stave it in. Everything had to be abandoned as quickly as it could be cut clear of the ship.

When all was done the poor captain sat disconsolate, I beside him, but unable to console him. The sad plight his beautiful ship was now in forced tears down his weather-beaten cheeks. The beautiful new ship which he had taken such pride in having put in such splendid order was a complete wreck, unable to proceed on its voyage. He was obliged to return to port to refit and face his owners, bringing them back a shipload of people to feed. A dreary night truly it was for the poor captain.

Morning brought a calm. A lovely sunrise shone upon a sea smooth as a mirror, in which was reflected the poor crippled barque. A small brig in sight answered our signals of distress, and a breeze springing up we were taken in tow until we could rig up a jury foremast and bowsprit, and get up some headsail to make her steer. Three days' fair wind brought us back to Greenock, *not* to the satisfaction of the owners, but they faced the situation energetically, for within twelve hours of our arrival our new figurehead was blocked out. The beautiful lady in flowing robes, which could be intended for no other than Zenobia herself, and which we had admired so much, was again to grace the bows of the ship. Fortunately for us there was a vessel on the stocks nearly completed, and the mainmast intended for it just came in to replace our foremast, and everything else in the same way which was ready for that vessel was handed over to us. In a word, we were refitted and off to sea again on the tenth day! During this time I suppose the passengers must have been praising the doctor—as well as the cow—to the owners, for on shaking hands with one of them on our second parting I found he had gilded my palm with ten bright sovereigns! I don't recollect it as a positive fact, but I should not mind betting heavy odds that I went to sleep in my bunk that night with quite a compassionate feeling of superiority— over the cow! Considering the heavy losses the owners had sustained, I could only look upon this present as a very marked appreciation on their part of my services on board. Well, I had endeavoured to do my duty, and a good deal more too, for in this world, if a man only does his bare duty, no doubt he will get on without much being said against him, but he will not get much said for him. It is the willingness to do more than is absolutely required from us that bespeaks sympathy from others and helps us along. I had tried to do all I could in my capacity of doctor, and being a youth of considerable method, I had, immediately on setting sail, promulgated a wonderful code of regulations regarding the due cleaning and scrubbing of the 'tween-decks, manner of drawing and cooking their provisions, &c., the result being that before the night of our disaster everything was going on like clockwork. When the owners came on board I suppose they saw my code hanging up, and appreciated the system I had inaugurated. The emigrants soon saw how it con- duced to their own comfort, and were willing supporters of the rules. The thing has all been now systematised, and even done according to law, but in 1839 the 'experienced surgeon' was left to his own resources, and much of the comfort of the passengers during the voyage depended upon whether he was a good administrator or not.

We had a most beautiful passage, not a gale of wind the whole way, and I was very fortunate in not having any sickness on board amongst my passengers. But all my skill, even aided and abetted by the valuable services of the inestimable cow, could not save two tiny children from pining away and being consigned to their last home in the ocean's depths. They were replaced, however, by two births, so when we arrived at the end of our voyage I landed my full complement of immigrants. We had long detentions at our first port of call. In those long-bygone days the facilities for discharging ships were conspicuous by their absence at such young settlements, and our pushing captain had to land the greater part of his cargo by means of the ship's longboat.

It was towards the end of the year before the *Palmyra* was an empty ship at the Sydney wharf and the experienced surgeon and the cow had respectively performed their duties, and had to bid farewell to their ocean home. The cow once more figured off in the newspapers, which was more than did the experienced surgeon. I was utterly eclipsed and completely thrown into the shade by the advertisement of 'A fine pure-bred Ayrshire cow' for sale on board the *Palmyra*.

The levee that cow held for several days was something to remember—and be proud of—for the cow. Streams of people came on board, but it ever was 'the cow —the cow' they asked for. Not one mother's son of them asked for the surgeon. The cow had it all her own way. If the 'experienced surgeon' had been appreciated at home by the owners to the extent of a gift of ten sovereigns at the beginning of the voyage, the cow was worth half-a-dozen times that sum to them at the end of it, which was more than could be said of the surgeon.

But there was no gainsaying the fact that in those days, whenever there was a case of 'pure-bred cows' *versus* 'experienced surgeons', the latter went to the wall. Any amount of demand for the former; the latter were a drug in the market. And so the cow one fine morning was marched away in triumph by the happy purchaser!

And the time had come, too, that I must march away —not in triumph! I had no friends in Sydney, had only one letter of introduction to a business firm, who treated me after a purely business fashion.

I was no worse, I rather think better off, than the youth who had been boasting of what *his* letter of introduction to the governor would do for him; for that exalted personage, holding up the letter between himself and the window, peered keenly through the missive and asked, 'Do they lithograph these things now?' I was spared that remark, at all events.

The kind captain allowed me to remain on board as long as I was in Sydney. The last day but one in the year of 1839 I shook hands with him and started in the mail-cart for Bathurst over the Blue Mountains.

I was off to connections away beyond the Bathurst Plains, away to the Lachlan River, to initiate myself into the mysteries of 'runs', 'maiden ewes', 'wethers', and 'stock' in general, to feel my way towards my new path in life, and determine my future career.

CHAPTER III

I Forswear the Great Convict Land

AS the mail-cart drew up at the little inn of Bathurst the clock struck the midnight hour, and the new year of 1840 was ushered in to me to the tune of a discordant fiddle, danced to by assigned convicts, who shuffled and scraped vile steps on the kitchen-floor to an audience whose well-marked countenances of the true convict stamp were new to me. I well remember going to bed with a disagreeable twinge passing through me, resulting from the question put in confidence to myself, whether I was quite sure that I *had* done the right thing in having exchanged my prospects in India for those in the land in which I now found myself. But in turning my back on the *Palmyra* I had finally disconnected myself with physic, and for ever barred the possibility of being ignominiously advertised in company with a cow! My future practice was never to be more than amateur, so to speak, only acting the good Samaritan when other doctors were not to be had. But that night I was far more in love with my profession than with sheep, and almost wished I had never heard of such a thing as a run in Australia. I really think the scraping of that fiddle and shuffling of those heavy feet, and the hoarse laugh which found its way to my bedroom throughout the night, created a feeling in me repugnant to casting my lot in life in a land where such an element as I had seen disporting itself downstairs existed.

Before morning my imagination—in the half-sleeping, half-waking state in which I lay—had conjured up a new and appropriate accompaniment to the fiddle—the clanking of the convicts' chains—but it was imagination only. The chained gangs I had seen working on the roads when crossing the Blue Mountains were not permitted to dance the new year in. That was a privilege only to be obtained when the chains no longer fettered them.

The morning of this New Year's Day was my first introduction to the day being ushered in with the bright sun of a midsummer's morning; but many and many more were in store for me in the future.

As I stepped forth from the little inn I looked on the Plains of Bathurst already basking in the hot sun. The convict element had disappeared—all was quiet! Last night's scene? Had it only been a disagreeable dream or a painful reality?

A bullock-team at this moment stopped at the inn-door, the driver entered, and from his face my eye instinctively went to his ankle. No, there was no chain there; but —last night's dream had *not* been a dream!

After breakfast I presented a letter of introduction to a gentleman in the neighbourhood, a retired military officer. He did not ask me if 'they lithographed these things now at home', but took possession of me there and then, installed me in his house, and set off to the inn for my light baggage. Under his hospitable roof I took my first lesson in dumping wool, for he was busy baling his clip to send down to Sydney for shipment home.

I had an opportunity also of studying the convict element of the colony—the population which supplied labourers for the settlers, for as yet the immigration which had taken place consisted mostly of capitalists who were employers of labour.

After a short sojourn with my kind friends I heard of a party of gentlemen who were going towards the Lachlan River, and I made arrangements to join them.

At that juncture it was prudent to travel in numbers, as

the country was infested by a gang of bushrangers who had been attacking the isolated homesteads of the settlers. Their mode of proceeding was something after this fashion: on arriving they collected all the inmates of the house, put them into one room, and placed a sentry with a loaded gun over them, with the instructions to shoot, without compunction, any recreant individual who dared to stir 'a —— inch', in the delicate language employed. This was termed 'bailing up'.

This ceremony completed, the gang then made free with the house and everything in it—took what they fancied and could carry away, which really was only money and jewels. They sat down and regaled themselves with the best to eat and drink in the house, and on taking their leave, whatever was better than what they arrived with, in the shape of horseflesh and saddlery, they took away—on the principle that a fair exchange was no robbery, the fairness not taken into account. The gang had been making quite a long and pleasant excursion, undisturbed by mounted or any other police, and were in full swing at that time. On our journey to the Lachlan River we had travelled just a day in advance of the gang, as they arrived at two of the inns in which we had stopped just the day after we had passed on.

I reached in due course of time, not the Lachlan *River,* but the river *course,* for the river itself had not been running for two years. The whole country was just recovering from a drought of unprecedented and alarming continuance—so that when at length rain fell, parents remarked to each other, 'What will the two-year-olds think of this?' for offspring had been born and lived to that age without ever having seen a drop of rain! On our journey we had had convincing proof of what the drought had been. We passed dried-up water-holes with circles of skeletons all around. Cattle and sheep had gone to drink, had stuck in the mud, and, without strength to extricate themselves, had there died. At the time of which I write, after rain *had* fallen, we had ridden for half a day at a time, looking forward to a drink of water at some customary watering-place, but on arriving at it found nothing more liquid than thick mud. We carried in our saddle-bags as many peaches as we could eat, and after eating one we kept sucking the stone to keep moisture in our mouths, the one peach and peach-stone keeping us going until we arrived at the stage where it was safe to indulge in another; calculating very nicely, however, the distance which so many hours' sucking each fresh peach-stone would carry us along on our journey until we reached our camping-ground of secured water supply. It was sometimes a shepherd's station hut, or the canopy of heaven, the latter the preferable of the two; sometimes a settler's comfortable homestead. From the Lachlan River I made another long tour, and in all spent three months travelling through the country, which gave me a perfect idea of that part of Australia and of the description of life that had to be led and the social intercourse that existed. And the conclusion that my sapient youthdom arrived at was that the whole thing would not do for me. I concluded that if I turned squatter and kept sheep, with my nearest civilised neighbour fifty miles off, and with only my fellow men of the released chain-gang to look at, the chances would be that I should soon lose the half-memory with which I had been born, and become little better than the sheep I had intended to own. And there was a still more cogent reason, and of a pecuniary kind—that most peremptory of all reasons—for my determining not to turn squatter—the price of stock was at such an exorbitant rate, some eight to nine pounds a head for cattle, and forty shillings for maiden ewes, that my small capital was nowhere. Add to this, moreover, that at this epoch of Australia's history the assignment system was done away with, so that the hitherto cheap free convict labour, which had been no inconsiderable element in the profits of wool-growing, had now to be replaced by free very dear labour.

My young mind, verdant as it most undoubtedly was,

could not see through these disadvantages which it conjured up, wisely as the future history of the colony proved. But the fact was that all this time there was an undercurrent at work. I had been harbouring one very strong predilection, one prevailing idea that *the* thing to do was to go to a new place and a new settlement, and rise with it.

My five hundred pounds would do nothing in sheep and cattle and farming in the existing state of matters in Australia. It might do a very great deal elsewhere in some other way in some other place.

I think if the real truth were known I had never got over or shaken off that first night's dream of shuffling convicts' feet and chained gangs, and unrecognised there still vibrated in my ears the discordant sounds of that vilely-scraped fiddle. And as I now knew of fresh fields and pastures new, where I *could* go and be a first settler, the slow but sure fever was at work which was to carry the day.

I determined to try my fortunes in the new land now proclaimed as pertaining to the Crown of England—a land where the taint of convictism was unknown, a land which the Imperial Government guaranteed should remain and be held intact from it, and to that land I determined to go.

And that fair land was Poenamo.

BOOK SECOND

The Town that Never Was

CHAPTER I

The King of Waiau

WE are sailing into Waiau Harbour.* It was known in the long-ago days of which I now write as Waiau, because Maori prevailed so much more than English that native names carried the day. Besides, there were but few places which had been christened in English, those only which had been named by the great circumnavigator. This will prove to you that I am writing of a time when Poenamo was just born to Great Britain, and was her youngest child!

What a fair and beautiful child she was, and how the youthful promise of her early years ripened into an adolescence which has brought worshippers to her shore from many and far-distant lands!

Where could be a brighter sky or more gorgeous colouring in land and sea, where could Nature more prodigally surround you with the beautiful in scenery, or give a more noble seaboard, or more lovely snow-crowned mountains clothed with richest verdure to their base? Where are grander fiords with glaciers from eternal snows sheer into the ocean, or lakes more picturesque and beautiful, or geysers—hot springs—warm lakes, solfataras like hers? And the fairy work, as if reared by an enchanter's hand, of her white and pink terraces, with ever-boiling waters streaming o'er—wonders that no tongue can describe, that the cunningest limner's brush cannot paint,

[* Coromandel Harbour.]

that no imagination can conjure up; the eye must gaze on the marvellous sight; from which none has ever turned away disappointed.

Such was the land of which I write—forty years ago.

We are sailing into Waiau and turning sharply to the left; in a few minutes we have dropped our anchor.

We are in a beautiful little land-locked circular harbour, but with hardly deep-water anchorage for more than half-a-dozen large ships to swing clear, though room enough for a large fleet of small craft. The shore shoals suddenly all round, where it meets the flat land at the base of the high range of hills forming the background; a steep range more than a thousand feet high, timber-covered to the very summit with evergreen foliage. Snow never falls on these hills. Between the spurs sloping down towards the shore are tiny, beautiful valleys, in which native villages can be seen nestling picturesquely. We are lying off a small island which forms part of the small harbour; we can see not far off a narrow passage between the island and the mainland, so narrow that I was often afterwards navigated across it on the back of a Maori *wahine* when none of the male sex were at hand. Abreast of us there is quite a pretty little bay and fine beach. We can see an incongruous collection of buildings, some weather-boarded, some evidently of native construction; then again there are quite a number of log huts, and there is the frame of a small craft on the stocks with all her ribs nearly completed. This little bay rejoiced in the name of Here-kino when I knew it in those days of yore.

And here lived and reigned the King of Waiau. The king was not a Maori king—he was a Yankee one, known as big W——* by the Pakehas, and as Wepiha by the Maoris.

Wepiha reigned supreme, not only in the harbour of Waiau, but along the whole shore of Te Hauraki, even unto the mouths of the Waihou and Piako rivers, if not

[* William Webster. Campbell spelled the Maori form of the name as *Waipiha*.]

a good way up them. Waiheke, Ponui, and adjacent islets owned his sway, and in not a few places utterly unknown to Pakeha the name of Wepiha was a power.

From whence this power, which extended over so wide a territory, came, I shall in due course explain.

Wepiha was a big man: he was, though a Yankee, as burly as a veritable John Bull. He was not only big in body but also in brain, whence came the retaining of the power he wielded, though not the power itself.

Wepiha had taken a wife—native fashion, and without the benefit of clergy—from the tribe of the great chief Taniwha, who could muster his three hundred—I don't mean wives, but fighting men. Under the shadow of the great Taniwha, who was known by the *sobriquet* of Old Hook Nose, from a certain resemblance to Wellington— under his shadow lived and reigned Wepiha.

But he ruled through the talismanic effects of two words, and throughout his dominions no two words were more often repeated by his subjects than the *whare hoko** of Wepiha. His strength lay in an unpretending-looking little building in one corner of Herekino beach—this *whare hoko*.

Yes, it was before the contents of Wepiha's store that the natives bowed the head and bent the knee!

Tell me not of missionaries as civilising agents compared to a *whare hoko*. The poor missionary could only raise on high his Bible and threaten the casting out into outer darkness, which the Maori in his early days of childhood had not learned to fear. But Wepiha, if a tribe offended him, simply shut the door of his *whare hoko* in their faces; he tabooed all his blankets and guns, his calico and spades, his cotton prints and tomahawks. It was terrible enough to have to stand this dire punishment, but when there was also included the ambrosial weed and the clay pipe, human nature could stand it no longer, and the proscribed humbly sued for pardon at the *whare hoko* door of Herekino that they might again be admitted

* Trading-house.

within its dearly-loved precincts and be at peace with its master.

Although Wepiha was a king of his own creation, he nevertheless did pay a small tribute—a sort of black-mail on the sly—to his father-in-law, who, in consideration of permitting his daughter to remain Mrs. Wepiha, periodically invaded Herekino whenever his stock of tobacco ran low, or he had broken his clay pipe. In fact, had King Wepiha adopted aboriginal customs and gone in for polygamy, an equivalent from out the *whare hoko* would have secured a plurality of wives, as well as covered any breach of the proprieties. To the Maori the word *utu*** covered any multitude of sins. True, amongst themselves, the word sometimes meant payment in blood, but with the Pakeha money or money's worth generally condoned everything.

Very nearly up to the date of which I am writing Wepiha had hospitably entertained any Pakehas who had found their way to his small kingdom. But Her Majesty, in taking possession of Poenamo, had caused such an exodus of land-sharks from Sydney that the King of Waiau all of a sudden found himself inundated with visitors to such an extent that keeping open house became too much for him. As public-houses did not exist, the king, to prevent himself from being eaten out of house and home, had no alternative but to convert one of the outhouses of his regal establishment into a barrack-room by fitting it up with bunks all round like a ship's forecastle.

And so he solved the problem of keeping open house by opening the barrack-door to all comers who chose to have the privilege of occupying a bunk therein, and a seat at the *table d'hôte,* and paying six dollars a week!

The current coin of his realm was the dollar. Wepiha being a Yankee, the whole thing fixed itself off in quite a natural way.

There was a grand promenade in front of the Herekino

* Payment.

establishment; it is true it was only a hop, step, and a jump from one end of the beach to the other, and, therefore, it did not take many persons, after all, to give the spot an animated appearance. It was on its wane when I first graced the promenade with my presence, and commenced paying my six dollars a week. An untimely blow had been dealt at the rising prospects of the *table d'hôte* at which Wepiha presided, and by the time I took my seat at it there was no scramble for places. In fact, the bulk of the sitters—Sydney land-sharks—had been completely dished by a proclamation issued by the Government, declaring that all purchases made from the aborigines after the date thereof would be illegal, null, and void. This thunderbolt had fallen shortly before my arrival, and evidently must have created a most disorganised and reckless frame of mind amongst the would-be land purchasers by latitude and longitude. Like Othello, their occupation was gone, and, awaiting the arrival of some chance vessel to bear them away from the disappointing pastures on which they had hoped to revel, they meanwhile found it hard work to kill time. The recklessness I have alluded to made a deep impression upon my juvenile mind, for I was young and verdant—very. I had seen little or nothing of the world. It was a small eye-opener to me when I put my foot on shore, for the first time, on Herekino beach, to be greeted by the sight of a knot of young fellows tossing for sovereigns! I am sure it was not more than five minutes after I had landed from the ship's boat that I might have been seen with not only my eyes, but mouth too, wide open with astonishment, when a sovereign fell upon the verandah-thatch over the barrack-door. The owner of that sovereign, too excited in his game, did not take the trouble to stop and look for the lost coin!

Such was my introduction to Herekino, the royal domain of King Wepiha. By the way, it was his black brother-in-law's prerogative to fish out and pocket that sovereign tossed on to the thatch. Not such bad diggings for him.

I have said that, to a great extent, the glory had departed by the time I arrived at Herekino, and the rapidity with which the beach promenade changed from being thronged with visitors to an almost deserted appearance was like the result of some magician's spell. Barrack-bunks were at a deplorable discount; the long *table d'hôte* became a mere mockery and a shame to poor Wepiha, who still sat at its head. Alas for the recipient of six dollars a week per visitor! he was at last supported by two pairs of *bonâ fide* intending settlers, a brace on either hand. The foot of the table faded away into an unoccupied distance dreary to behold. Of course I was one of the four supporters of the now-dethroned *table d'hôte* king. But I must say he bore his dethronement with a right royal grace, genial, jovial, brimful of good-humour, of a temper simply imperturbable as a Maori. A Pakeha with the Pakehas, a Maori with the Maoris, was this great John Bull of a Yankee, so like an Englishman, although an American. Of his antecedents it matters not; the only thing I ever heard whispered against him was that he had run away from his whale-ship; whether a friendly mate lowered his tool-chest into the boat he escaped in he best knows, but he had first wielded his axe in the forest before he developed into the King of Waiau.

I speak of him as I found him—a fine, right-hearted, easy-going, kind fellow, with plenty of brains, and knowing how to use them. He had worked himself into quite a fine trade, such as it was in those days, preparing cargoes of timber, buying pigs, potatoes, and maize from the natives, and shipping this produce off to Sydney and Melbourne to feed the too-rapidly-arriving immigrants who were flowing into Australia in 1839-40. I remember my fancy was tickled the first time I ever heard the King of Waiau's name, for it came about after this manner: The ship in which I reached the Hauraki was in command of a skipper who knew not the land nor its shores nor the waters in the gulf, so we went creeping up Hauraki, looking for Waiau, and sunset found us half-way up to the mouths of the great rivers at the head, when we could do nothing but drop our anchor. Next morning, just after we had got under way, we saw a whaleboat bearing down upon us, and laying to, we were hailed with the question, 'Is Mr. Wepiha, the pig-merchant, on board?' What a designation for the King of Waiau! He wasn't, of course, but we got the inquirer to come on board and pilot us into Waiau.

One day at dinner we had something to talk about, for a schooner had arrived from Kororareka, bringing us the last news from the Government headquarters there, and we were discussing whether or no, in our wise opinion, the governor's future town would be a success. We were busy also discussing a remarkably fine boiled leg of mutton and caper-sauce, which *was* pronounced an inimitable success, for Herekino boasted a *chef-de-cuisine* who had once worn his white paper cap of office on board the great smack service between London and Leith before steam drove them off the face of the seas. This so disgusted the *chef* that he swore roundly at civilisation, and betook himself to the antipodes thereof. I found him exercising his genius in serving up the hind leg of a pig so cleverly skinned and trimmed with caper-sauce that the King of Waiau carved it round to us all as—mutton!

We were all as loud in our praises of the *mutton* as we were loud in our censure of the governor for fixing himself at such an extremely northern out-of-the-centre place as Kororareka. Why had he not come to such a grand locality as Te Hauraki, with its grand rivers flowing into it, and fixed the capital there? Wepiha listened in silence, no doubt saying to himself, 'Much you greenhorns in the land know of what you are talking about, as if there were no other better places than Te Hauraki', and he let us expend our quartett wisdom.

We were four cannie Scots, and were all four hardly a match for one shrewd Yankee. Ponderous Wepiha, when we had expended our talk, quietly put in his oar by saying

'The mouths of the Waihou and Piako might be capital places for wild-duck shooting and mosquitoes', but he knew a better place, rather, he guessed, for a capital, and *that* was the point at issue.

There was a something in the manner in which he gave utterance to this that caused a simultaneous 'Where?' from us all to echo through the room.

But the king for the moment gave no response. He had just filled his mouth with the last morsel of skinned hind leg of pork-mutton, and we saw by the deliberate way in which he put his knife and fork down on his plate, and still more deliberate manner in which he consigned that last mouthful to the capacious but now well-filled receptacle which was to receive it, that the king was about to deliver himself of something in the way of speech beyond his common wont.

'Wait till you see the Waitemata.'

These were the words he spoke and all that he said, but the words were so oracularly spoken that we all held our breath, staring expectantly at the oracular spokesman for some further wonderful revelation.

But he spoke only, and repeated slowly, these words: 'Wait until you see the Waitemata.'

CHAPTER II

We Start on the Exploring Expedition

THERE was an unusual bustle one morning on Here-kino's now-deserted beach, and it was about a week subsequent to that dinner in which I had been initiated into the mysteries of how to make a leg of mutton with caper-sauce out of the unclean animal, and when Wepiha had fired our imaginations by his oracular enunciation of 'Wait until you see the Waitemata'.

Herekino beach seemed awakened from the sleepiness into which it had so sadly and permanently dropped, and as if it were reviving the bygone days when grand land-hunting expeditions used to start therefrom. To the land-sharks Wepiha gave a certain amount of line to play with, just as much as suited his purpose and no more, for when-ever they ran off in any wrong direction that interfered with himself he landed them safely on the bank of some native difficulty or other, which he had no difficulty in creating mentally and declaring as an existing one!

The bustle at Herekino on this occasion arose from a land-hunting expedition of Wepiha's own originating, and we were starting to go and see the Waitemata.

It had all been discussed and settled. We were off on an expedition which was to result in the making of all our fortunes. Downright inheritances for our very children's children were to be forthcoming from it, not to mention handing all our own five names—the sapient originators'—

down to posterity. Wepiha had fairly infected us with his
enthusiasm for the Waitemata. In the most glowing
colours he had depicted the extent and magnificence of the
harbour, the beauty of its sloping shores, the richness of the
land on the isthmus—for there was still another harbour,
but it opened on to the opposite or west coast. Wepiha had
not received an education which made him conversant
with any more classic Corinth than the one he had heard
of in his own Yankeeland, or no doubt he would have
made his glowing descriptions still more glowing by
telling us he was going to show us an isthmus more beautiful still and more grandly situated than even the Corinth
of the ancients. If it had not a high rocky Acropolis it had
its towering extinct volcanic crater, which commanded
the two seas and looked down upon both. But I must not
anticipate. You will learn all about it in good time, but
first we have to start, and then we have to cross the gulf,
and by the time we have done that I shall be at the end
of another chapter at least, but not at the end of our
journey.

The native crew have launched the boat down the
beach into the water. A fine stalwart crew they are, who
can pull an oar and feather it just as well as they can
'paddle their own canoe'. They are carrying the requisites
for our expedition down to the boat in great glee and good-
humour, for they always enjoyed going with Wepiha in
any of his visitations to his trading stations, or on excur-
sions such as we were about to make.

The day was a glorious one. Nature had robed herself
in her brightest and sunniest of colours, and the gentle
breeze just rippling the water gave promise of a fine and
smooth passage across the gulf.

The reader of to-day may perhaps be wondering
whether in our equipment we had provided ourselves with
firearms. No, not with an arm of any kind, save plenty
figs of tobacco! These constituted the arms with which
we should be able to repel all attacks upon us. With plenty
of that 'shot in the locker' we well knew we could both

fight and pay our way through the length and breadth of the land. These were the happy piping times of peace, when the country was literally ruled by the power of pipes and tobacco. The Pakeha was much too valuable an animal in those days to be killed and eaten; that game did not pay at all. Cannibal feasts did come off now and again on the sly, but the Pakeha was too dear a morsel, and, moreover, was far too salt to be put into a *hangi* (native oven) for epicurean Maoris. The native-grown-and-fed article was not only the cheapest but nicest; it was not too salt.

Alas! in later years it came about that the aborigines fell away from the good taste of their earlier bringing up, and then came the epoch when 'cold missionary on the sideboard' did prevail!

I have already stated that we were a Scotch quartett headed by a Yankee, but whether the word 'cannie' was applicable to any of us time will reveal; all I know is, we were all under the delusion we were wondrously smart clever fellows. As I was the youngest, I have no doubt I considered myself quite the cleverest of the lot! Of course I cannot paint my own portrait to you, nor is it necessary that I should do so with regard to two of my fellow-countrymen, but the fourth was in every way a man of such peculiar ways—a character—and as he has long ago taken that long excursion which we must all take once, *he* cannot look upon his own portrait, unless, indeed, he can through some spirit medium, and then he will see it has been painted by a kind and friendly hand.

Cook—for so I shall designate him—had numbered his thirty summers, and the outward form and manner of the man revealed a good deal of the inward nature. He was most particular in his dress, and on the beach at Here-kino, where a free-and-easy style of costume prevailed, he always appeared in strong contrast, and looked as if he had just been kidnapped from Regent Street without having been allowed to alter his costume, so little did it or the wearer seem to belong to the general surroundings. The black cloth coat, the stiff and elaborately-tied neckcloth, and the black chimney-pot hat always made him look as if he had dressed himself for some particular occasion to pay or receive some visit of ceremony; and but for the fact that one knew quite well there was no one with whom any visits of ceremony could be interchanged, one could never have got over the inclination to say, 'Hallo, what is Cook dressed for?'—it took some time to get accustomed to the fact that this was his natural state. His conversation and manner of speaking were after the same fashion as his dress—very set phrases, with grand and peculiarly expressive words, often, it is true, used for very trivial subjects. He had most indomitable perseverance and great energy of character in his own quiet, determined way, and once engaging in any undertaking he would go through fire and water rather than be beaten. If he ever espoused the cause of a party, or the quarrel of a friend, he would stand by them through good report and through evil—desert them never.

The boat is nearly ready, and we have all got our odds and ends on board save Cook. This morning our worthy friend is not the Regent Street swell of yesterday. He looks as if he were just starting for the moors on a 12th of August, but he is still the same precise, stiff-looking person. He is standing on the beach close beside the boat, and at his feet are arranged a row of ever so many small boxes and little bundles, and not until he has ticked them all off upon his list does he allow them to be put on board by the crew. Cook liked to rough it just with as many little comforts as it was possible under the circumstances to take with him. I had brought a nice little lined tent with me to the colony, and as we were taking this with us, Cook anticipated quite a pleasure excursion, for we should not be compelled to sleep in native huts, always disagreeably over-populated, making the Pakeha *flee* from them when he had the chance. If we got beyond the sheltering roof of native huts, no doubt we might have fallen back upon the resource—one not to be despised either—of a sail stretched over an oar for a ridge-pole, and so improvised a tent after a fashion, but with a nice comfortable lined tent Cook did not see why he should not take along with him comforts to match, so he had made his preparations accordingly.

We were all having a quiet joke at his expense and poking fun at him as we stood on the beach ready to start, declaring that so much baggage could only be accounted for by the hypothesis that he had a hidden supply of female attire, and that some hitherto unknown Mrs. Cook must be going to take us by surprise and make one of the party.

Cook entered into the fun and carried on the joke against himself, but he kept a wary eye to see that all his little treasures were duly and carefully stowed away in the boat.

We were quite a large party as we settled down into our places in the boat. There was the king, tiller in hand, and one of his Pakeha traders whom we were to leave at a station in passing, we had four Scotch 'cannies', a young native boy (Cook's page!) and a crew of eight—no fewer than fifteen in a rather small boat. In fact, we were little more than a streak clear!

We push off from the shore and are in deep water. Look on shore. Do you see that funny-looking bundle of blankets on the beach with a black topknot? Scrutinize it more closely and you will discover it to be a head of black hair, a forehead, and a pair of eyes! That is Madame Wepiha seeing her lord and master *pro tem.* away. You can see a good many bundles of blankets and black top-knots scattered over the beach, all immovable. That is the native fashion of bidding good-bye, and as we pull away from the shore many voices are heard to say, *'Haere, haere'*, and from the boat is wafted back the response, *'E noho, e noho nei?'* 'Go, go', is the word of farewell. 'Stay—stay there, won't you?' is the reply. Such is the native manner and custom. They do not shed tears when parting from each other; they do so when they meet after a long absence. I may have an opportunity hereafter of explaining how

c

this comes about according to Maori philosophy, and I can assure you their conduct is based on perfectly sound philosophical principles. But meanwhile we must *'haere'* along or we shall never get clear of Herekino.

CHAPTER III

We Sing and Row Ourselves over the Hauraki

WE have rounded a headland and shut out of sight the great Wepiha town. The crew settle down fairly to their oars, and we are pulling through the harbour entrance, and have opened up the Hauraki Gulf. We are making straight for the opposite shore, and heading for the northern point of Waiheke, high land which we can see distinctly some fourteen miles distant.

The day is magnificent, not a cloud to be seen, the sun shines down with a genial warmth, it is a dead calm, and the sea as smooth as a mirror, and as flat as one too, for no swell comes in from the open sea: we might have been in a millpond. And very lucky it was we had such weather, for had it come on to blow even a moderate breeze we should have been compelled to lighten the boat, and poor Cook's *impedimenta* would have found a watery burial, and some of ourselves a grave.

The Maoris pulled well and lustily, keeping time with their oars to a song which sometimes had one word, sometimes two, as a chorus, which the crew took up and repeated as they pulled the oar out of the water. These boat-songs were very often improvised, all save the refrain, and when the Pakeha was a passenger, generally referred to him. All the native village gossip of the day, whether social or political, came to light in these extemporised boat or canoe songs; and if any new scandal was on the *tapis,* it was jubilantly given forth in terse and unmistakable language. The Maori being an intense gossip, has an insatiable curiosity to know everything that is going on, and generally does manage to know.

The best authority in native circles, and from whom the best supply of gossip was drawn, was generally one of their own young chieftainesses, wedded for the time being to a Wepiha or other Pakeha. I ought to tell you that in those old lawless bygone days the chiefs generally made it a condition that the Pakeha who took up his quarters with them should be respectably wived—that is, according to Maori custom—and the Pakeha had to accept matrimony as one of the conditions on which he was allowed to locate himself. The Maori reasoning was simple as conclusive— the Pakeha once wived, he had then no excuse for paying attentions beyond his own legitimate *whare!* Oh! sound Maori knowledge of human nature!

This was my first experience of a native crew and of their songs, but many were the songs I had heard both in boat and in canoe ere the half-Maori, half-Pakeha settling of the early days had passed away, and became exchanged for purely Saxon manners and customs.

And now the crew are improvising as fast as they are pulling, each rower, one after the other in rotation, giving a line, and all repeating the refrain at the end of it.

I got Wepiha to translate their song to me as it was sung, and I find it amongst my old manuscripts thus converted into doggerel the same night before turning in:

> The white man wanders in search of a home,
> Far from his country and friends does he roam.
> > Tena Kūmea!
> He came o'er the water to visit our isle,
> And when he beheld it his heart did smile.
> > Tena Kūmea!
> Our country is good where *kumara* grow,
> And clear sparkling waters constantly flow.
> > Tena Kūmea!

He came to our chiefs to purchase some land,
And blankets and guns he brought in his hand.

> Tena Kūmea!

For a price. we gave him a planting ground,
Close by Waiheke in Hauraki Sound.

> Tena Kūmea!

And now he wishes to build a large *pa,*
And goes to buy land from great Ngapora.

> Tena Kūmea!

Yet for our village the Pakeha sighs,
And swears that for Kora he lives and dies.

> Tena Kūmea!

Ah, Kora, thou hast caught the white chief's heart,
And chained him to us with thy cunning art.

> Tena Kūmea!

In this manner, when at the oar, the natives take free licence in commenting on any of the Pakeha idiosyncrasies and having a sly hit at them, and the more especially if the Pakeha proclivities have taken the direction of admiring any of the village native beauties would it be exultingly proclaimed. The allusion to Kora, I discovered from Wepiha was aimed at Cook, who, at the conclusion of the song, when the last long prolonged *kū-me-a* had died away, thus delivered himself:

'These savages must always concoct some ribaldry or other of that kind. What a noise the creatures make! Europeans would do twice the work with half the row.'

One of Cook's peculiarities was to run down the Maoris. He had come to the country expecting to find them a very easy race to deal with, whereas in his land speculations, and, indeed, in everything else, he had discovered they were as acute as they were intelligent, very ready and willing to sell bad land at a good price, but always displaying a sturdy obstinacy in not selling good land at any price at all.

Cook's remarks, therefore, on the simple aborigines might be held to savour more of the sour grape order than anything else. Wepiha, on the other hand, always stood up manfully for Tangata Maori.

'Come now, Mr. Cook', he said, 'don't be running down the natives because that young lady's name was brought on the carpet. You can't deny these young fellows make capital boatmen, and will work well for a whole day at the oar, happily and cheerfully, and never grumbling one bit. For my part, I would never think of exchanging them for white men.'

'Ah! but then you forget you have yourself turned half-native. I almost expect to see you take to a flax mat, bare legs, tattoo your face down to the very tip of your nose, and forget how to speak your own language. I am morally convinced you are fast coming to that, and when you do arrive at that delectable condition I promise you to forego all my prejudices against the Maoris in so far as to hire you as one of my boat's crew, granting you free liberty to improvise at your oar and deal in personalities to your heart's content.'

'Ah well! There is no saying what I may be reduced to yet. I shall take a note of your offer. But come now, between ourselves, confess, does not your aversion extend more to the male gender than the female?'

But before Cook could make any reply to this insinuation, the crew, who had been taking a spell of quiet rowing, again broke out into song:

Ah, Kora, who gave her that beautiful gown?
Te-na!

E hoa* Cookie, why do you frown? *Ku-me-a!*

A Pakeha came to our *pa* one night, *Te-na!*

And next day appears Kora in clothes so bright.
Ku-me-a!

Ah, Kora, she wants a Panama hat. *Te-na!*

Te Cookie will surely give his love that. *Ku-me-a!*

How pretty she'll look in her new *potae,†* *Te-na!*

With love in her heart, and thanks in her eye.

* *E hoa,* Oh friend.   † *Potae,* cap or hat.

All end in a prolonged shout—'*Hu-u-a!*'

'There now!' exclaimed Cook, 'that is just a sample of the kind of stuff your favourites indulge in.'

'All very fine to call it stuff', I said, 'but I rather imagine some of these little boxes of yours "could a tale unfold" in the shape of feminine apparel if examined. I have heard, I think, that Waiheke is famed for the beauty of its native ladies.'

'And evidently you think they are all purchasable for a few yards of printed calico', retorted Cook.

'Or a Panama hat; and ten to one I'll find one in this little box of yours', said I, appropriating the one nearest me, and commencing to open it.

Cook indulged in a quiet kind of snigger to himself while I was opening the box, but it did not escape me that when all were watching what I was about to disclose, he adroitly got hold of the only other box at hand and put it safely under the boat's thwart behind his own feet, so that no one could get hold of it.

'Well', said he as I was in the act of opening the lid, 'turn it out and let us all admire the new hat, or perhaps it is a gown done up in a small compass.'

'A key-bugle, I declare!' I exclaimed, not a little surprised, and taken rather aback, as were all the others, for we had never heard its notes blown on Herekino beach.

'Ah well!' I said, 'we shall let you off the opening of any more boxes if you will only cheer us up with some music. Come now, something appropriate: "The King of the Cannibal Islands", or, perhaps still more appropriate, what would you say to "Love lies bleeding"?'

Cook took the instrument, put it to his lips, breathed through the bugle, touched all the keys, giving his hand a jerk upwards as he put it to his lips, and just as we expected to hear the first note ring out and float along the smooth waters, he suddenly stretched out the other hand, and seized the case, and before we knew what he was about, the bugle was safely replaced, the box closed, and it was put under the thwart to keep the other box company.

When Cook said 'No' in this pronounced and practical manner it was a decision *à la* Cook, final and irrevocable, so not another word was said, Wepiha merely remarking:

'Well, you must sound our approach when we near the *Delhi,* for I am going to leave you all on board whilst I go on shore to see how my Maori workmen are getting on in dragging down the cargo; the last log was to have been in the water to-day.'

The *Delhi* was a barque of some 500 tons which he was loading for the Australian market, for in those days Waiheke had many a stately *kauri* growing on it.

As not a breath of wind had sprung up there was no respite to the rowers, and well and lustily they gave way to their oars. Occasionally they would rest for a minute or two and refresh themselves with a drink of water from a calabash, and then pull away as vigorously as ever, and as we had two spare hands the crew had a spell by turns.

Wepiha chatted away with them during any intermission of their songs, as he wanted to post himself up about the chiefs of the tribe with whom we should come in contact, with reference to the object of our expedition.

The boat at last neared the opposite shore, and as we were passing round the point of a small islet Cook took out his bugle, and the notes of a rather startling blast were echoed from the steep shore ahead of us, and all at once we opened up a passage between the islet and Waiheke, and we saw the *Delhi* at anchor in the fairway channel with a large raft of timber at her stern.

On coming alongside, Cook's warning notes having heralded our approach, we were welcomed, after a sailor's fashion, by the captain, who was only too glad to encounter any one who would relieve the monotony of his situaton, and give him news of the outer world.

After dinner it was discovered that it would be too late, on Wepiha's return from visiting his timber-draggers, to proceed farther on our journey that day, so we determined to accompany him on shore, and return again and spend the night on board, and make an early start of it the next morning.

CHAPTER IV

The Timber-Draggers : A Pull for Dear Life

THE western shore of the Hauraki Gulf is studded with numerous large islands and chains of smaller ones. Between some of these there are fine deep-water channels which form sheltered roadsteads for large vessels, one alone being large enough for the combined navies of the world to ride at anchor in.

The *Delhi* was lying in one of the lesser roadsteads, at its entrance from the gulf, for the convenience of being in the immediate vicinity of the timber-loading ground, so as to save distance as much as possible in towing off the rafts. But for this consideration the vessel would have lain a mile farther up channel, and this would have sheltered her from the north-east fetch, to which she was now exposed. The reasons for my being particular as to the *locale* will be apparent before you have read to the close of this chapter.

The row across the gulf had so whetted our appetites that the captain of the *Delhi* had no cause to complain that we did not do justice to his hospitality. When Wepiha declared that he must leave us at our wine and be off on shore to visit the forest we begged off from our host too, so that we might have an opportunity by accompanying Wepiha of seeing the timber operations in the bush. Borrowing the ship's dinghy, we pulled ourselves ashore, leaving our native crew to rest on board. We landed to the welcoming cry of '*Haere mai! Haere mai!*' from a large assemblage of the Maori feminine gender. What males there were, were of such tender years that they were of no account. The grown men, and the half-grown too, were all in the forest dragging out the last large log for the vessel's cargo.

As we passed through the native village, nestling in a little valley at the base of the high land, we noticed that the women were all busy preparing food, and the preparations were of rather an extensive kind, the fact being that as the last log was expected to reach the water's edge this day the timber-draggers were going to be regaled with a sort of small feast, and as no wars had lately been going on, giving a war supply of animal food, a virtue was to be made of necessity, and the modern substitute of pig was to be the order of the day.

In the days of which I write Maori ladies did not flaunt in the last new fashion—or say the second last—from Paris, but if they were less fashionably they were far more picturesquely attired. Their flax mats and the blanket folded around their persons formed drapery which hung gracefully around them, and in which they looked natural and at ease, and, unencumbered with shoes and stockings and accompaniments, they moved about gracefully, *cum grano*. At all events they did not look as if they were going to topple over, as they do now when clothed in those troublesome disguises which we wear, and balancing themselves on high-heeled boots. 'Tis true we should have preferred that some of the old hags we saw scraping potatoes and *kumara* had been somewhat more disguised. The short mat from waist to knee only exhibited to our view their 'ugliness unadorned displayed the most'! But we had just to put that against 'beauty unadorned adorned the most', and, rolling them together, accept the average as it came out before us.

We were soon surrounded by a small band of native infantry—say up to five years—in that simplicity of clothing ascribed to our first parents *before* their fall when fig-leaf aprons had *not* been invented. Those of maturer years had some rag of a garment about them, native or imported.

Our guard of honour piloted us skilfully, first skirting for a short distance the level land where it met the hills, then, striking off at a right angle, conducted us at once into the forest, and we had not proceeded very far before its silence was broken by the distant shouting of a large body of men, the sound reaching the ear at regular intervals as if keeping time to, and joining in, a chorus. A short distance farther into the forest, and then through an opening in the trees the native workmen came into sight, and their wild song struck loudly and startlingly on the ear.

It was a wild and exciting scene. The huge log the natives were dragging out was of unusually large dimensions, some three feet in diameter and some eighty in length, the largest spar of the *Delhi's* cargo, and the last required to make her a full ship. Every available man of the tribe had been mustered to drag the spar out, and then feast afterwards. The head of the spar was decorated with branches of flowering trees, and waving tufts of feathers had also been fastened on, adding to the effect of the 'head-gear'. At this decorated end of the spar, and on it, stood the oldest chief of the tribe. Round his waist he wore a short mat of unscraped flax leaves dyed black. It looked like a bundle of thatching more than anything else as it hung down to his knees. This constituted his whole attire. In his right hand he brandished a *taiaha*, a six-foot Maori broadsword of hardwood, with its pendulous plume of feathers hanging from the hilt. High overhead he brandished his weapon, imparting to it the peculiar Maori quivering motion, with outstretched arm raised aloft, like unto a soldier leading on his men to battle. He kept repeating a long string of words in quick succession, lifting up one foot and stamping it down again, the body thrown back on the other leg. Every moment his voice became louder and louder until almost reaching a scream;

then he grasped the weapon with both hands, sprang into the air, and came down as if smiting an enemy to the earth. At this instant some eighty or more men, minus a flax mat like the chief, or even fig-leaf, yelled forth one word as ending chorus. As one man they simultaneously stamped on the ground, and then gave one fearful pull on the rope doubled round the end of the spar—a pull that you thought would snap the rope in two; but it stood the tremendous strain, and the huge mass forged ahead several feet. The chief sprang into the air again, flung his arms on high, yelled out a word, the gang repeated it with a louder yell, the earth almost vibrated, as, springing into the air, they landed as one man; then another strain, and away slid the spar a few feet more. Again and again this is done, the old chief becoming more and more excited, and even more agile instead of less so, his voice attaining to a higher and higher key until he positively screeched, and after each tug the spar advanced several feet. At last, after one tremendous pull, the gang ended their shout by prolonging it until it died away in a comparatively softened tone, and the chief accepted this as an intimation that they must have breathing-time before beginning again. So they rested; meanwhile a tribe of young children brought kits full of wet mud to besmear the sleepers in front of the spar to make it slide along more easily. It had only to be dragged a few hundred feet farther when it would be launched down a declivity to the sea-beach. So we took a stroll farther into the forest to see the trees in course of being felled and squared for other cargoes. This allowed time for the draggers to get the spar over the intervening space, as we wished to see it make its last long swift descent down to the water's edge.

On getting back again we were just in time to hear the old chief begin his long recitation to work the men up to proper pitch. This he did, and after some vigorous strains on the rope we saw the branches, flowers, and tufts of feathers suspended, as it were, in mid-air; then the other end of the spar tilted up, and away rushed the stupendous mass, sweeping everything before it, snapping young trees like carrots, and then passing clear of the forest it flung a cloud of dust into the air as it swept across the narrow belt of open ground, pursuing, like an avalanche, its wild career, and by the time the prolonged shout with which it had been sent on its last swift journey had died away the spar had reached the beach, and its garlanded head, now sadly despoiled, sent a shower of spray into the air, showing it had reached the water's edge, and then another loud, long, and joyous shout rang through the forest.

Nota bene.—The old warrior chief was *not* standing on the end of the spar when the last long and strong tug at the rope was given!

Surrounded by the natives—no longer nude now that their work was over—we retraced our steps to the village, at which I shall leave our native friends to enjoy a Maori feast without describing it here, as I shall hereafter have a more fitting opportunity. The sun was now fast sinking, and we had to get into our little dinghy and pull back to the *Delhi*.

Wepiha seated himself in the stern and took the tiller, we took the oars, and we soon pulled out from the bay into the open reach. With the evening a smart breeze had set in after the hot, calm day, and we found we had to pull against a strong tide and a strong wind. The short, bluff little boat bobbed up and down in the jabble of a sea, the spray dashing over the bows. We were half-way from either shore and a good half-mile from the ship.

And now the tide ran swifter and the wind blew stronger, and we amateur rowers pulled weaker just when we were wanted to pull stronger. And when the nose of the little boat plunged into the head sea you thought it was never coming out again, and the spray literally went right over us, flying slap into Wepiha's face as he sat in the stern-sheets. We were soon all soaked to the skin, and the water in the boat began splashing about our feet. On looking towards the shore through the gloom the painful truth was forced upon us that instead of gaining ground we were losing way. I was but a poor oarsman in those days, and feathering my oar was an accomplishment I had still to learn. If I had only known it I had plenty of hard rowing before me.

Darkness closed in upon our struggle, the shore loomed up a black mass, but fortunately for us we had a beacon light from the stern cabin windows of the *Delhi* to steer by, and we strained away at our oars to reach our desired haven.

'Lay in the after oar and bail out the boat', sang out Wepiha; 'she lies like a log in the water, and we are not making a foot headway.'

So now, to make matters worse, we were only three at the oars, and had to strain away harder than ever, but though we did so, and for ever so long too, the beacon light grew no brighter or nearer.

'Why, there is more water in the boat than when you began to bail', I exclaimed. 'I feel it up to my ankles now.'

'I thought I had made but little progress', said Cook, who was bailing, 'considering how long and hard I have been at it.'

'Off with your hat and bail with it', I said. 'That broken calabash is no good. The boat has sprung a leak, and the water is gaining upon us.'

'Pull, my boys', shouted Wepiha. 'Well done! A strong pull, a long pull, and a pull all together. Steady stroke and we'll soon make way.'

But the way we made was very doubtful, and the water kept swashing about our legs, and was ominously plentiful, though Cook was bailing away like grim Death—and for fear of him.

'Stick to it, my hearties', cried Wepiha when a lull came, 'stick to it. I dare not put the dinghy round to run before it; she would be swamped before I got her round. Stick to it.'

Of course we did—we redoubled our efforts. Stick to it? Yes, I should think so, for grim Death was having a hungry look at us, and we pulled, and pulled all together, to keep him from boarding us and taking us to his eternal haven. We had no desire to reach it just yet. We were not sick of life, and we had our worldly eyes on the *Delhi*; that was the haven we wished to reach, and her beacon light seemed to mock us. Stick to it? Didn't we just! We were all too young and the world *was* still too dear for us to leave it yet awhile.

Yes, we strained our utmost. The wind still blew as fiercely, but fortunately for us the tide had slackened, and we did make some headway. Then a fiercer blast came, and we barely held our own. But the still-slackening tide favoured us, and during the lulls we at last made visible progress, and Wepiha cheered us up by proclaiming how distinctly he now could see the lights from the *Delhi's* stern windows.

At last, drenched from head to foot, and with blistered hands—mine were, at all events—we reach the *Delhi*, and scramble up the rope-ladder. The welcome voice of the captain said he concluded that we had remained on shore, or he would have sent a boat's crew to our assistance.

This was my first struggle for life on the waters of Poenamo—but it was not destined to be my last.

In blanket bay we all slept soundly that night on board the *Delhi*—all the sounder for having stuck to it so well. And had we not stuck to it so well we should have slept under the waters of Te Hauraki!

CHAPTER V

The Night Camp : The Morning's Vision

W E had intended to make an early start in the morning when we rose none the worse for our hard pull and sound drenching of the night before, but whoever has had to do with Tangata Maori well knows how one's temper is tried by that irritatingly provoking word *taihoa**. I had not then become acquainted with that word, but the day was coming when the word would be written in my still young brain—written there indelibly and for ever.

And the old age which has overtaken me has *not* erased from the tablets of my memory the Maori *taihoa* engraven there now forty long years.

To those of easy-going and lymphatic temperament, *taihoa* was not a red flag that maddened, but it was to the quick and irascible.

I don't consider it would be fair to set down a man of my comparatively angelic temper as irascible, but I am free to admit I have just anathematised *taihoa* in confidence to myself—yes, ground my teeth and muttered words too horrible to be spoken aloud—words at which one would shudder in calmer moments—drawn from the hidden depths of a vocabulary unknown under any other provocation. Oh! the relief and ease it was to oppressed nature when the drawled-out *ta-i-ho-a* fell upon the ear,

* By-and-by, [wait awhile].

just as if it mattered not one jot whether the thing need-
ing to be done were done then, at some future time, or
not at all, and that even to relegate it to a future was a
waste of brain-power only worthy of an untutored
Pakeha who knew not the true philosophy of life, and
was steeped in benighted ignorance of the ineffable
luxury of a *taihoa* life!

Wepiha was equal to any amount of *taihoa*-ism, and
Tangata Maori loved him accordingly. If there had been
fifty-two weekly judgment days he would have waited
until the very last rather than stop a Maori saying *taihoa*
—would have waited with the patience of one content to
have the tobacco-pipe of *taihoa* peace passed from a
Maori's lips to his own. Superhuman patience! How often
did I not covet it!

Wepiha had been doing so much *taihoa* that morning
that it was eight bells before he got back from the native
settlement to the *Delhi,* where the rest of us were impatiently waiting for him to return, so that we might
start again on our journey. Then when he did come it
was not worth while starting when it was so near an
early dinner-time which the captain made expressly for
us, so now we all did *taihoa* together—and, in fact, we
played our part so well at it that when we ordered the
crew into our boat to ship the masts and set the sails it
was just within a couple of hours of sundown.

The truth was, a fine fair breeze had been our temptation to dawdle away the time doing justice to the hospitality spread before us in the *Delhi,* and as we were in
ignorance of the length of our intended journey, and
where we were to encamp for the night, we had to
believe Wepiha when he kept repeating, 'Oh! *taihoa,*
plenty of time'.

But at last we did get away, and when pushing off
from the *Delhi's* side the captain hailed us with a *'Bon
voyage!* and don't forget that I am to have my choice
after you are all satisfied'.

I don't think we replied to him 'All right', for I think

that extensively-embracing answer was not invented then, but we assented to the captain's parting reminder with a 'Very well, we won't forget'. We spanked along under our two spritsails with a fresh breeze after us, having Ponui on one hand and Waiheke on the other, and after running some half-dozen miles we turned sharp at a right-angle and opened up the roadstead waters of Prince Regent's Inlet, so named, not by Cook, but by a navigator of later days*. As we rounded the point we could see at the farther extremity of this sheet of water, in mid-channel, a small island with a high hill, and for this Wepiha steered. It was some fourteen miles distant. The wind blew pretty fresh, and we sped along at a good pace, but before we got half-way the sun set, and a dark starless sky was overhead, and it looked threateningly squally. No improvised singing from the crew reached our ears.

Te Cookie had no sly innuendoes poked at him, but we did hear a plaintive *sotto voce* kind of strain coming from the bow of the boat, where the crew lay huddled together in their mats, half of them smoking their pipes. The sail was but a dreary one, and as we kept peering through the increasing darkness the little island's little mountain kept looking as provokingly far off as ever. We were to have encamped on the mainland beyond the island, but when Wepiha said he could pilot us into a nice little bay in the island where the boat could lie sheltered from the strong east wind which was now blowing, we all voted he should steer us to the island, as the sooner we landed and could pitch the tent for the night the better. It was of some moment to be able to anchor the boat safely, as, unless we were able to do so, she would require to be emptied of everything, and hauled up on the beach.

We were sailing merrily along, and at last the island loomed up close at hand, and Wepiha informed us he must make a sweep round to avoid a nasty reef which

[* Named after the *Prince Regent* schooner, 1820.]

formed part of the shelter of the bay for which he was
steering, so we hauled in our sheets and put the boat in
the wind, and just as Wepiha told us we were safely
round the reef, bump we went, and we were safely on
top of it, with a very nice little sea bubbling round us!

'Is this the beautiful little bay where you were to put
us on shore so comfortably?' asked Cook in his blandest
tone of voice. 'I really cannot congratulate you. I fear it
will be rather wet to walk on shore here.'

'It will be rather wet sitting in the boat', said I, 'if
it gets a few more bumps like these.'

'We'll be all right in a minute,' said take-everything-
easy Wepiha; 'I'll soon put her into deep water again',
and seizing a boathook he helped the crew, who had
slipped out of their blankets and into the water, to prevent the boat drifting broadside on to the waves, while
they held her up by the gunwale and waited for a wave
to get her over the reef. After one or two good hard
thumps we were safely over and in deep water, the
natives making a sudden jump on board as we slid off
the reef.

We had to douse sails and take to the oars and pull
out again, so as to get clear of the whole of the reef. The
night was very dark, and Wepiha confessing he had lost
his reckoning of the precise locality, made a virtue of
necessity, and when fairly clear of the breakers around us
put the rudder down, left the island astern, and again
made a fair wind of it by running the boat for the mainland, putting us into a beautiful little sheltered bay—a
most diminutive one it certainly was—with a nice sandy
beach right under a bold headland,

It was fine deep water, and we all soon jumped ashore
from the bow of the boat, and then set busily to work to
carry up everything out of the boat on to the little narrow
strip of land between the beach and the cliff. We had to
haul her up above high-water mark in case of a change
of wind during the night, for although the bay was quite
sheltered from the easterly wind then blowing, it was
not protected from other points.

The little tent was soon pitched by some of us, others went fern-pulling, so as to carpet the floor of the tent and make it comfortable for our beds, others went firewood-hunting, and as the spot was familiar to some of the natives they knew where to go for fresh water. A large fire was soon blazing, and on it a goodly-sized three-legged gipsy pot full of potatoes, kumara, and a lump of corned pork, also a small pot with water for making our tea.

We were at last all sitting round the bright blazing fire, which kept burning freely owing to the strong breeze; we were waiting until tea was ready—all save Cook, who was busy inside the tent. Flinging down great armfuls of fern anyhow for a bed was not Cook's idea of the thing at all: 'nothing like method' was his axiom, which he kept ever inculcating, and now he was acting upon it after a practical fashion—he was 'methodising' his bed. The fern being large, some six feet long, had of course rather thick, coarse stalks. Now half-a-dozen of these coming together and not covered by anything would have made too hard a rib under Cook for him to have slept comfortably upon, not that he would not have eventually fallen asleep, and soundly enough too, but he certainly would have lain awake accusing himself of not having carried out his 'nothing like method' principle, and feeling that he was justly suffering punishment from the ribs of fern for his dereliction of duty. Cook was now busy securing himself against any such chance of not being able to tumble luxuriously off to sleep the moment he laid himself down in his bed—according to *method* of course. The plan he was pursuing was simple and effective—and worthy of imitation by those who were constituted *à la* Cook—for all that he did was to place the fern in consecutive layers as if thatching a roof, and to carefully cover the stems with the softer fern-tops. And truly, if you but use plenty of fern, a bed thus made of freshly-pulled fern is simply most deliciously luxurious, a fine springy softness unrivalled by any patent modern invention. But Cook's bed did not end with fern only; he spread a strip of native matting over the fern, and then we saw disgorged out of one of his wonderful packages veritable sheets and—a feather pillow! It was a small one, certainly, but Cook's square foot of feather pillow no doubt caused him, when he pillowed his head upon it, to smile with a comfortable reflection of how little it takes to secure comfort if one only takes the trouble to do things in proper methodical manner.

This style of travelling of Cook's was all very well with water-carriage and pitching a tent on the beach, but it would have taken an army of pack-carriers to have done inland trips *à la* Cook. The base of Cook's land-purchasing invasions had always been from the Waihou and Piako Rivers, which accounted for his baggage-train having assumed anti-pioneer settling style, and savouring of effeminacy. I was destined to know the day when civilisation on that very shore robbed me of luxurious fresh fernbeds, and yielded me no comfort in lieu thereof.

By this time the Maoris were making their preparations for the night, and it was evident they expected a stormy one, for they brought the boat's sails on shore, and with an oar or two extemporised a tent for themselves, one quite sufficient to protect them from rain, which from these preparations they evidently expected, otherwise they would have been content to sleep, rolled up in their blankets, under the canopy of heaven.

We were now all grouped round the fire, some standing, some sitting, some lying on the ground, Pakeha and Maori intermixed. Ever and again someone would fling some dry driftwood into the fire, and it would spring up into a brighter blaze, illuminating the whole diminutive bay. Jutting out into the sea on either hand was a high bluff, crowned with overhanging evergreen trees, and the camp fire burned so brightly that every limb was clearly seen, almost every leaf distinguishable. The little plot of level land on which was our encampment, the steep bank covered with fern six or eight feet high, up to a perpendicular ridge fringed with brushwood, were all thrown into bold relief by the background of dark sky overhead. The little white sandy beach, the boat, the surface of the water lighted up near at hand, and then imperceptibly fading away and lost in the murkiness in the rough waters beyond, all formed a scene wild yet picturesque of its kind, and could it have been flashed by some magic mirror before the eyes of the relations and friends of those who formed the foreground, they would have gazed upon it with intense interest. If the truth were told, however, I don't believe there was one of us who at the moment had artist eye enought to appreciate the picture we made.

Alas! our eyes were turned towards the contents of the large pot on the fire; for substantial as our dinner had been on board the *Delhi,* we were all ready to do justice to the boiled corned pork, potatoes, *kumara,* and cobs of maize that we impatiently waited for the pot to disgorge.

In due course of time we had all plied a good knife and fork to our fare, only the fork was conspicuous by its absence; each used his own clasp knife in those travelling days, and forks the over-fastidious Cook improvised from the forked branch of a neighbouring shrub!

One after another we took refuge under the canvas roof of the snug little tent, and, covering ourselves with our blankets, were soon in the land of oblivion. I remember, however, that I first watched Cook getting under his sheets according to method, but after what fashion he courted sleep remained to me an unknown thing, as I dropped off first. No doubt he slept according to a rule and method which forbade such a wasteful proceeding as to wake during the night, for when a downpour of rain awoke me, Cook was slightly snoring and sleeping the sleep of the innocent. The rain came down pretty smartly, and was the tail of the north-easter which had been blowing, and which the natives had wisely provided against by converting the boat-sails into a tent.

The morning broke divinely with a bright blue sky;

not a vestige of bad weather; all clouds cleared away. Before starting, the inevitable pork and potatoes were consumed, with a pannikin of tea, and an early hour, when the sun was not much above the horizon, saw us pulling out of the little nook of a bay, leaving it to resume its solitude unbroken, for this was the first time it had been broken by Pakeha man. Just as we rounded the headland, Wepiha exclaimed 'Behold the Waitemata!'

And well he might tell us, as he did on that night when he presided at the Herekino *table d'hôte,* 'Wait until you see the Waitemata'.

Ah! never can I forget that morning when first I gazed on the Waitemata's waters. The lovely expanse of water, with its gorgeous colouring, stretched away to the base of Rangitoto, whose twin peaks, cutting clearly into the deep blue sky, sloped in graceful outline to the shore a thousand feet below. Still farther distant we saw a bold round high headland, backed by a still higher hill, and far away before us a long expanse of glancing waters as far as the eye could reach. Behind us basking peacefully in the morning sun lay the little island, and the reef off which we had been bumped by Wepiha the night before. The little island we could now see in all its beauty, with its crater hill, and through the broken lip we could get a peep into the crater itself. How silent and peaceful were Waitemata's lovely sloping shores as we explored them on that now long long ago morning! As we rowed over her calm waters the sound of our oars was all that broke the stillness. No, there was something more—the voices of four cannie Scotchmen and one shrewd Yankee (the sum and substance of the first invading civilisation), loud in the praise of the glorious landscape which lay before them. On that morning the open country stretched away in vast fields of fern, and Nature reigned supreme. It is fern-clad now no longer, but green fields gladden the eye; the white gleam of the farmer's homestead dots the landscape, there are villas on the height, and cottages on the shore. White sails skim along the water, and the black smoke can be seen of many a steamer as it cuts its way, passenger-laden; and last, but not least, but loudest, with its screech of civilisation, the locomotive on the iron road proclaims, 'I have reclaimed the wilderness and made the desert place glad'.

I little thought on that morning that I should live to see such marvellous changes—the wildest fancy could not have dreamt of them. Over how many miles did a clumsy locomotive run in England in 1840?

We rowed up the beautiful harbour, close in-shore. No sign of human life that morning; the shrill cry of the curlew on the beach and the full rich carol of the *tui* or parson-bird from the brushwood skirting the shore fell faintly upon the ear. The sea was smooth as glass, and the flood-tide swept us along. In half-an-hour we reached the mouth of a deep bay, which Wepiha pronounced to be that of Orakei, and turned sharply to the left and made for the head of it, and, as it was high water, we were able to land at a small shelly beach at the base of some lovely wooded slopes*.

Here we found signs of human habitation, for Wepiha had steered us to where there was a native settlement, but we found it empty—not even an old woman, the customary guard, left to protect the vacated premises. The huts were all locked up—that is, the doors were tied up with a strip of flax-leaf, a quite sufficient 'barrin' o' the door' to keep out all intruders save enemies on the war-path, but from them even the old woman guardian would not have been safe, for although she might have been too old and tough to eat, she would nevertheless have met her doom.

Wepiha at once concluded that the tribe were on the other shore of the isthmus shark-fishing, and if we wished to get hold of them we must face a two-hours' walk. As we did want to catch our Maoris we determined to start at once, but as we were to return to spend the night here, we first took the precaution to pitch the tent, so that the

[* This landing-place was near the head of what is now known as Hobson Bay.]

crew could have our fern beds ready when we came back.
If we were late in getting back we should thus have
nothing to do in the way of preparations for the night on
reaching our camping-ground.

So we turned our backs on the Waitemata, and taking
a winding path leading up through the wooded slopes,
we shaped our course for the natives' fishing village on
the opposite shore of the isthmus, for Wepiha told us he
was now going to show us another grand harbour which
opened on the west coast, and we were about to cross the
isthmus to reach it.

CHAPTER VI

The Isthmus of Corinth of the Antipodes

BEAUTIFUL was Remuera's wooded shore, sloping gently to Waitemata's sunlit waters in the days of which I write. The palm fern-tree was there, with its crown of graceful bending fronds and black feathery-looking young shoots; and the *karaka* with its brilliantly-polished green leaves and golden yellow fruit; contrasting with the darker, crimped and varnished leaf of the *puriri,* with its bright cherry-like berry. Evergreen shrubs grew on all sides of every shade from palest to deepest green; lovely flowering creepers mounted high overhead, leaping from tree to tree and hanging in rich festoons; of beautiful ferns there was a profusion underfoot. The *tui,* with his grand rich note, made the wood musical; the great, fat, stupid pigeon cooed down upon you almost within reach, nor took the trouble to fly away. There was nothing to *run* away from us; for Nature, however prodigal in other respects, had not been so in vouchsafing any four-footed game. Fish in plenty, fowl but scanty, flesh none, save a rat, so poor Tangata Maori had to fall back upon himself when the craving for animal food seized him, and thus it may perhaps be inferred that land squabbles had ofttimes a *belli*cose origin in more senses than one, and that the organ of destructiveness was called upon to administer to that of alimentiveness, and cannibal feasts were the result.

But Tangata Maori's transition epoch had already set in. He now sometimes donned a shirt under his blanket, though the restraint of a pair of inexpressibles was still unknown to him and still a thing of the future. Pigs, thanks to circumnavigator Cook, were now plentiful in the land, and cold missionary had become rather a dainty dish. As for smoking, if a Maori had only tobacco enough his pipe was never out of his mouth, so he was making slow but very sure steps in the march of civilisation. And here were we deliberately planning to erect a town on the shore of the Waitemata, and thus place him in the very centre of seducing temptations, with the pure and disinterested motive of reclaiming him from his savagedom and hoping whilst doing so to receive our reward in the manner we wished. We were now in quest of the owners of the soil to see on what terms we could acquire it. We had not taken long to decide that Wepiha's praises of the Waitemata were not exaggerated, and on no more fitting shores could a township be located. And it appeared to us on that bright and lovely morning that no town could lie on a more beautiful spot than the slopes of that shore. As we gained the summit of the ridge and turned to look seaward we stood entranced at the panorama revealed—stood entranced in mute amazement at the wonderful beauty of the glorious landscape.

Yes, we had come on this excursion site-hunting! We were going to purchase a modest tract of country and supply impatient intending settlers with town, suburban and country lands to their hearts' content, or rather to the extent that their purses would give power of paying. Castles in the air which we had been building of rapidly-amassed fortunes seemed to assume a palpable reality now that Wepiha had unfolded to us the grand and beautiful isthmus which we were now traversing. Well justified was he, truly, in having said at the Herekino *table d'hôte* in mysterious yet oracular tone, 'Wait until you see the Waitemata'—we came, we saw, and we were conquered. Without one dissentient word we succumbed; we

now all swore by the Waitemata, and were jubilant exceedingly as we walked along the native footpath, the high
fern and *tupakihi* proclaiming the richness of the soil.
An hour's walk brought us to the base of a volcanic
mount, some five hundred feet high, rising suddenly
from the plain, the name of which Wepiha told us was
Maungakiekie, but as it had one solitary large tree*
on its crater summit we christened it 'One-tree
Hill', which forever obliterated the Maori name from
Pakeha vocabulary, but the grand old tree has passed
away, causing later-day arrivals to wonder why the hill
bears its name. Alas that native names should have been
replaced by Mount Eden, Wellington, Hobson, Smart!—
as if *we* were that smart people who would have changed
them to Mount One, Two, and so on. And the islands in
and around the harbour had better have been called
A, B, C Islands, rather than change Motu-Korea to
Brown's Island. What a blessed thing that Rangitoto has
escaped the sacrilege of being named forever as perhaps
'Two-Pap Peak Hill'! Had it been smitten with such an
indignity the very name would have marred the beauty of
that island's lovely outline, and the landscape would not
have been the same with such hideous words paining the
ear. And why not say Remuera instead of Hobson? Great
heavens! *Hobson* as against Remuera—Selwyn's Failure
as against Kohimarama! What's in a name? Everything
—the rose wouldn't smell as sweet by any other, just
because imagination is more than half the battle, and our
senses ever befool us unwittingly. But I must retrace my
steps to the base of Maungakiekie, and where we first
looked down upon, and felt the fresh breezes from, the
western waters of the Manukau, these opened up to our
sight resembling a great inland lake hemmed in by the
sea-coast range of high forest-clad land. Through a break
in the range—the entrance, in fact, to the harbour—we
got a glimpse of the sea on the west coast. Underneath us,
away at the foot of the slope which stretched from where

[* A *totara*. In later years other trees were planted there.]

we stood to the shore, close to the beach we could see the
blue smoke rising from the native settlement to which we
were bound. We walked slowly down the winding, sloping footpath, endeavouring to understand the topography
of the landscape which revealed the headlands of both
the east and the west coast, interlacing each other in a
manner so puzzling that we were unable to unravel them
and know which were which. The cool southerly wind
blowing over the great Manukau basin we inhaled with
positive physical enjoyment. In after-life I have only
known such crisp delicious air when on alpine summits
or Highland moorlands in early autumn with the first of
the clear northerly winds. As we neared the settlement
we walked through a large *kumara* plantation, and upon
coming near the huts and being descried by the natives
were welcomed with the customary cry of welcome,
'*Haere mai, haere mai!*' and waving of their mats.

We had arrived most opportunely; the steam was just
arising from their *hangi* as these were being uncovered,
and we were all soon served, each with a little freshly-
plaited flax-leaf basket filled with most deliciously cooked
kumara, potatoes and *peppy* shellfish* The native oven I
shall describe in a later chapter, when you will find me
living amongst the Maoris in a native village; the oven is
a simple contrivance whereby a kit of *kumara* or an
entire Maori can be cooked with equal convenience—and
well cooked too!

We had not yet got to our journey's end, however,
although we had stumbled on so good a dinner *en route,*
for the chiefs of the tribe were on the opposite shore of
the harbour at their shark-fishing. We saw around us
plentiful proof of their takings, as shark was hanging up
to dry in the sun from lines stretched from pole to pole,
and the odour therefrom was not of a too pleasant description. Our repast finished with a draught of the most
exquisitely clear spring water which gushed out on the
beach in a wonderful stream. We got into a canoe and

[* Pipi.]

paddled over the narrow passage to the other settlement or fishing station*, and at last found we had fairly run our game down, and stood confronted with the old chief Kawau, and a young one of note by name Te Hira, of whom I shall soon have somewhat to tell you.

We propounded the object of our visit—that we were not pig but land hunting, and furthermore that we had set our hearts on the Remuera slopes stretching down to Orakei Bay. But to the question, would they sell that land, a very prompt and decided *'Kahore'* (No) was unhesitatingly given, but they would sell land farther up the harbour.

And for many a long year these Remuera slopes remained native-owned, and to this day part of Orakei Bay still is. And so we paddled back again, the chiefs accompanying us, for after having had such a long chase to find them we deemed it safest to bag our game there and then. We—the four 'cannies'—left Wepiha to do some trade *'korero'* with the natives and follow after us along with the chiefs, whilst we at once started on our return —by the same path we had come that morning—back again to Orakei.

As we reached the base of Mount Remuera, which the footpath skirted, I proposed that we should venture a scramble to the summit; but of the other three cannies two were too cannie to face it, Cook and Makiniki making straight for our camping-ground, whilst we 'ither twa' braced the hill. It was pretty stiff scrambling over the top of high fern; for sometimes, when unable to creep through it, we had to trample over it as best we could, but at last we gained the crater-top.

Ah! I shall never forget the feelings of gratified amazement with which I gazed on the wonderful panorama which lay revealed to my sight for the first time on that now long-ago day. 'Age cannot wither nor Time stale' its infinite beauty in my eyes. Since that day I have travelled far and wide, have stood on the Acropolis of

[* At Mangere, Manukau Harbour.]

Corinth and looked on *its* isthmus and sea on either shore. I have seen Napoli La Bella and didn't die, have gazed on panoramas from alpine and Apennine summits, but in later years, when I again stood on that selfsame spot on Remuera's Mount, and gazed across Waitemata's waters and its many islands to Rangitoto's Peaks and the Cape Colville Range, I confess that to me it surpassed all I had ever seen elsewhere—stood forth pre-eminent, un-equalled, unsurpassed*.

The sun now dipping behind the western coast ranges, and warming up in reddening glow Rangitoto's Peaks, warned us it was time to descend from our high estate in order to reach before it became dark the little tent which we saw as a white spot away down on Orakei beach. Regaining the footpath, we sped along down the slopes, and soon were enjoying a pannikin of tea which we found ready on our arrival at the camp.

Before very long Wepiha arrived, accompanied by the chiefs who on the morrow were to point out the land which they would be willing to sell. We did not allow the night to grow very old before the heaps of fresh fern upon which we had spread our blankets wooed us to luxurious rest.

I wot those of us who did not sleep too soundly even to dream, dreamed of a fern wilderness suddenly con-verted into a smiling town, and down its handsome streets, by some strange confusion of ideas, we were all paddling in a canoe steered by Wepiha and the bottom of the canoe was well ballasted with bags of gold.

On that night, now forty years ago, the large Pakeha population—five all told—slept on Waitemata's shore for

---

* This panegyric received confirmation a score of years after it was written. Two travellers making *le tour du monde*, not *en quatre-vingt jours,* stood upon a spot where a much more circumscribed view of the same landscape lay stretched before them, and, just as a friend of mine passed them, the one exclaimed to the other, 'Well, Harry, after this the Bay of Naples may shut up!'

the first time—of Maoris I know not how many, but a large number.

And after the passing away of forty more years, who can tell how many Pakehas shall sleep on Waitemata's shore, but will there then be Maoris in number five all told?

Who can say?

For then fourscore years will have been numbered in the past since the first arrival of that Saxon race before which the coloured man inevitably disappears. For here there is no undiscovered country to which he can retreat and hold his own. He is face to face with that civilisation to which he succumbs.

He is inclosed within a limited area, with a seaboard penetrated by innumerable harbours, with a fertile soil, with a climate the most genial the world knows, and by its speedy occupation he will be crowded out.

For this land of which I write is destined to be the happy pleasure-ground of all the Great South Lands of the Pacific.

CHAPTER VII

The Mess of Pottage which floored the King of Waiau's Grand Scheme

WITH the morning came a damper to our spirits, for when we rose we found a hard south-easter blowing, with the unpleasant accompaniment of rain.

The Maoris consoled us, Job-fashion, by saying there would be three days of it, and as Wepiha rather agreed with them, we made up our minds to accept the situation and make the best of it. We commenced to do this by moving to the native village, where the largest and best *whare* was placed at our disposal, and we all respectively arranged our own allotment of space according to our ideas of what the occasion required. One great point was gained by the exchange from the little tent to the much larger hut: we had some room in which to move about without knocking each other's elbows at every turn. What we did not gain—an immunity which the tent did give us—was freedom from certain jumping insects. The tent, pitched on virgin soil and carpeted with fresh fern, was free from the disagreeable visitors, which were always too numerous in Maori *whares*. But there are other places besides the uncivilized Maori hut where it is impossible to be rid of *that* annoyance. In the most civilized spot on the earth—of ancient days, whatever it is now —in the Eternal City, in these modern days, those who have dwelt there know how futile is the attempt to be

D

rid of these plagues. In church and galleries they swarm; in the very streets as you walk along they take possession of you, and ruthlessly attack you. If you wish to keep one little spot in your apartments clear of them—your bed— you must remember never to throw any of your clothes upon it when returning home from your day's sight- seeing, but to hang up everything in another room, and thus you may at all events mitigate the constant annoy- ance.

We found these gentry so lively in our new quarters that they made our enforced imprisonment almost un- bearable; however, we had to make the best of it. We had not a book among us. Wepiha, being able to talk Maori, had a resource we could not avail ourselves of, for he could set a chief on an old war-path story and listen to the stirring tale of how warriors had not only fought but eaten each other—I mean, of course, the survivors ate the others! We could not even indulge in an innocent game of pitch-and-toss just because we had not one coin to jingle against another. Our small change, and large too, was represented by figs of tobacco. With these we paid our way. No pitch-and-toss—no books—no cards—no anything—a Maori hut, a blowy, rainy day, and four stolid Scotchmen thrown on their own resources, for Wepiha was deep in the past history of Maoridom. Such was the state of the case, and what were we to do to kill time?

An inspiring Providence moved me thus to deliver myself, and unwittingly solve the problem:

'I say, old King of the Cannibal Islands, can't you invent something better for our dinner than that ever- lasting pork and potatoes of yours?'

'Just thank your stars you ain't a Jew, my boy, and that as yet your teeth are about as long as your beard. No fear whether it is pork and potatoes or potatoes and pork, I'll warrant you'll play a pretty good knife and fork.'

'No such articles in the whole civilised establishment, O king! but if you can't forage better I'll promise to be up to proper appreciating mark even in the consumption of the unclean beast. But really, can't you do something better for us?'

'That is all according to taste. If you fancy a pigeon cooked on a split stick before the fire, this is the season for them. I don't know whether there are any, though, in this bush.'

To his inquiry the reply of the natives was that the cry of the *kukupa* had been heard.

'Then it is all right', said the king. 'Let the cook prepare, for pigeons you shall have just as sure as you are sitting there.'

Wepiha was quite justified in thus asserting that pigeons we should have, for though they were at this moment in the bush still unshot, they would just as certainly be in our pot before an hour was over.

To Waitemata cockneys of to-day it ought to be explained that the *kukupa,* now no longer to be seen on those shores, was just the bird created expressly for the true cockney sportsman—the one after his own heart. What a rage poor *kukupa* would create could he be only imported within sound of Bow Bells with his own peculiar aboriginal habits! What safe and glorious sport he would make, to be sure! for if not brought down by the first shot, why he only shakes his feathers and calmly waits to be shot at again!

Little wonder that Wepiha declared 'pigeons we should have', but a little hitch did crop up nevertheless, for all the *tupara** (double-barrel guns) were at Mangere, and there was only one old 'Brown-Bess' forthcoming, and a few ball cartridges! But Tangata Maori was quite equal to the emergency. He walked down to the beach, searched for some stones as small as it was possible to pick out, and so primed with the munitions of an uncivilised sportsman he sallied forth, the rain notwithstanding, to bring us Wepiha's promised supply of pigeons.

* Maori pronunciation of 'two-barrelled'.

It may be all very well to say in a civilised cookery book, 'To make hare soup, *first catch your hare'*, but such a direction was not needed by those making *kukupa* soup at Orakei Bay. Just as sure as there was the water already boiling, so sure was it that *kukupa* would go into it, for Wepiha had said they made capital soup, as well as a grill, if you had only plenty of them. Well, we had plenty, for the number the sea-beach small shot gave us was fifteen. Poor stolid *kukupa,* how we blessed the stupidity of your nature that rainy day! You killed the day for us, if the day killed you. I ought to have mentioned the one cautioning entreaty with which Wepiha had sent forth the emissary of death to the *kukupa*—if he found them sitting on the low branch of a tree not to put the muzzle of the gun *quite* close to their breasts, or he would be sure to blow away all the fine fat, and this was wanted to be consigned to the pot as well as the rest of the bird, for this fat would be a prime element in enriching the soup.

The truth of the old saying, 'Too many cooks spoil the broth' was now to be tested, for we all went heart and soul into the great work which was to help us to kill time, and we were as amused as children with a new toy. It was not that the other old saying, 'Small minds are easily amused' was about to be illustrated; we all had brains enough to set at naught the application of *that* adage to us, but we had nothing else to do, and when people have nothing to do they very often begin to think of what they will have for dinner more than befits intelligent beings. We were in that sad predicament.

The wind still blew and the rain came steadily down, so that there was no going outside the hut. Fortunately it was quite a large and a lofty one, and we could stand upright without sending our heads clean through the thatch, so we had reason to be thankful for some small mercies. We were thus able to prowl round about the fire whereon boiled our three-legged gipsy pot, in which two brace of *kukupa* were cooking. But a brief time ago they had sat on a *puriri* tree, cooing and eating the ripe red berries. We all had a turn at the soup-making; some put *kumara* into the pot, some put *taro,* a vegetable which is like a lump of flour, and if left long over the fire boils away by slow degrees and thickens the soup. Wepiha had sent a boy to collect some young shoots of wild cabbages. These were put into the pot; then he popped in just a tiny bit of the everlasting corned pork—just enough to salt and make more savoury the whole contents.

The pot boils briskly; the *kukupa,* which, if they were happily mated and in melting mood, wooed each other in the leafy shade not long ago, give promise of being very tender—after another fashion.

The pot boils briskly no longer; the *olla podrida* has grown so thick that the *kukupa* toss and tumble no more, but are stewed up in a closer nest than ever they had before. The pot now simmers in faintest murmur, and seems sinking into an apopletic slumber from very repletion. We all sniff the delicious aroma from afar, for we watch it close at hand no longer; we are lying at our ease on our flax mats, our mouths in watery expectation of that mess of pottage on which we are about to feast.

We little dreamt then what the *débris* of that mess of pottage was going to bring about after we had partaken of the bulk of it. Happy ignorance!

'It must be ready now', a voice was heard to exclaim suddenly and in an impatient tone, and the exclamation found a responsive echo from all the other cooks!

The *chef-de-cuisine* who had thus spoken was Cook. He was seen to walk with most dignified composure towards the one object of attraction, and the *chef* behaved like a man: he boldly tasted the concoction!

We remained in breathless suspense and anxiety, for the *chef* uttered not a word. What! had that savoury odour deceived us? After all our loving care was it going to be a failure—a mockery and a delusion? Was our day to have been spent in vain? Saints of Maori-ism forbid! The *chef,* true to his character of staid deliberation, exercised it on this grave occasion beyond his ordinary wont, and gave no visible sign of how his palate had been affected. At last in solemn accents he proclaimed, 'It wants one thing more', and then suddenly turning round and betraying excitement by the quickness of his movements—for him—he went to one of his wondeful little boxes, and taking therefrom a bottle, poured half the contents into the steaming pottage, and solemnly exclaimed—

'With this ruby wine I christen thee "Orakei Ragoût the Incomparable".'

The dread spell under which we lay was broken, and we all jumped up with a hurrah!

Many, many years are gone since that *ragoût* was christened the Incomparable on the then silent shores of the Waitemata, years which brought to some of that party a bright and happy fulfilment of their youthful aspirations—a bright and beautiful summer to their hopes and expectations of the future, to others but a chilling spring, and to others but a dreary winter, for so 'runs the world away', and we have to play our allotted parts.

But to us all there remained a remembrance of that *ragoût* as if it *had* been the 'Incomparable', a delicious feast over which we had all been so joyous and happy in the Maori *whare* of Orakei.

O mess of pottage! but for thee man might have asked, 'How are lots in Cooktown?'

Oh! amateur cooks, why ate ye not up that *ragoût* to the last sop in the pan? And why left ye one for others to quarrel over?

Fatal mistake! When we could eat no more we stopped—at least when we thought we could not eat any more; but had we only known what was about to happen we would never have admitted such a supposition; we would have eaten that *ragoût* to the very scrapings of the three-legged gipsy pot itself! Alas! it was thus it fell out:

Cook's native attendant, when we had finished our grand repast, appropriated the unconsumed remainder. But one of the young chiefs of the tribe, Te Hira, who had come to be a party to the intended sale of land, considering he had the best right to the spoils of his own territory, made a grab at the *ragoût*-pot, when Cook, standing up for *his* boy, interfered and asked Te Hira why he was *tahae*-ing the *goahore**. He meant '*taking* away the pot', but in his imperfect knowledge of the language he used the word *stealing*. So Te Hira retired to nurse his wrath, and we found on the following day he had nursed it to some purpose. The weather-prophets had made a miscalculation, and instead of our having three days' rain the next morning broke fine, so we pulled away up harbour looking at all the bays and the pretty shores, and ever asking, 'Won't you sell this and that and the other?' and it was always '*Kahore! kahore! kahore!*' and we pulled away almost to the headwaters of the harbour until we came to an island called Pahiki [now called Pine Island], with only a narrow boat channel to get at it, and this choice spot Te Hira *would* sell. But it was ourselves, and not the land, he was 'selling'; for Wepiha, getting hold of some of the other Orakei natives who had come with us, soon found out that Te Hira was in the sulks. He had been called a *tahae*†, and he was only leading us a dance, and he would not consent that any land should be sold, and it would only be a fool's errand to go any farther.

And so there was nothing for it but to turn our boat's head the other way and just 'gang back ag'in' with what grace we could. In the afternoon we had landed the Orakei natives at their settlement, and the wind being fair we proceeded on our way, *not* exactly rejoicing, and after dark reached the *Delhi,* and there spent the night.

And the next day, after getting a thorough drenching in crossing the gulf from the heavy sea running, and

[* *Kohua,* a pot. Early traders and whalers variously rendered this word as 'goahore' and 'goashore'.]
† A thief.

just being able, running close-hauled, to reach Waiau, we township-site-hunters arrived at Herekino to the merry blast of Cook's bugle, for by this time we had all recovered our spirits and had been laughing over our wild-goose chase.

And thus it fell out that men never did ask, 'How are lots in Cooktown?' for that town never was!

BOOK THIRD

With the Maoris on the Hauraki Shore

CHAPTER I

Why we Invaded Waiomu

BUT time, tho' slow, is strong in flight, and years rolled swiftly by, saith a fine old song which I used to sing in the days of my youth, and truly Time slacks not his pace, but swiftly courses along, and with the passing away of twoscore years hath my youth also passed away.

Yet how vivid still the remembrance of that year of grace 1840 when I first learnt a settler's experiences on the Antipodean shores of Poenamo, with life's young dream all before me, creating glowing visions of the future, *couleur de rose* on all sides! There were no dark shadows falling anywhere on the bright picture conjured up by an imagination ignorant of the world's battles which had yet to be fought!

Ah, the *châteaux en Espagne*! how fearlessly youth builds them, and what noble structures come to an untimely end!

Happy delusions! what were life without them? How they entice us along, bright hope leading the way! What though realisation fades away, and 'like the baseless fabric of a vision, leaves not a wrack behind', what though 'Hope told a flattering tale' and it was a fiction only—a reality never. Did not the fair goddess lead us over pleasant pastures, and did we not pleasurably disport ourselves for the time being? 'What a little day of sunny bliss' was ours! Still we had it; it was ours. Ah, thrice-blessed Hope!

Having now blown off my prefatory steam to my Book the Third, I suppose I had better proceed to practical work without more ado.

In my last sketch I introduced you to quite a civilised little spot on the Hauraki Gulf, where twoscore years ago a *table d'hôte* was daily spread, and I told how the spreading thereof had died a not natural but quite a sudden death, and how its once great glory had departed until the King of Waiau had only four subjects (and these Scotch ones) left to support his presence. And now I have to chronicle the sad fact that the king was left absolutely alone in his glory, for of his four last subjects two had already winged their flight and the other two were now bidding farewell to Herekino, and starting on the race of life on their own account.

I am not going to write one word of fiction. Even as 'The Town that Never Was' told only a simple story of actual fact, so 'With the Maoris on Te Hauraki Shore' facts only will be narrated.

To those who have ever lived amongst the natives, what I am about to set down will read 'stale, flat and unprofitable', but there is now here so large a population who know not Tangata Maori nor his manners and customs, and who can have but a faint idea of how the first settlers had to find their footing in the land before any permanent settlement had been established, to whom the actual life-pictures I am about to portray may be a new book containing matter all unknown before, that I would fain rescue from oblivion the chivalrous conduct of the Maori when his power was supreme, towards the invading Pakeha.

Cooktown was a thing of the past and of the imagination; we had sown our township speculation wild oats, and awoke to a more sensible frame of mind, and to the inevitable quarrel which would have arisen with the Government had we been so bold as to have laid out an independent township and sold it off in their very faces. True it would not have been difficult for us to have done this, but it would have been quite impossible to have given the purchasers of our town lots a clear title, and in default of this the speculation would have come to grief. The Maoris would have maintained Wepiha in possession of any purchase he made from them, but that would not have served the purpose, for people won't buy land unless with a transferable title, and that most assuredly would not have been forthcoming. Our wild excursion only proved how even the most sensible of men can be led away at times!

But though the idea of lots in Cooktown had died away from our creative brains, the remembrance of the glories of the grand Waitemata waters lived there, never to be effaced from the memories of the two who had scrambled to the summit of Remuera's Mount and looked down therefrom.

That a town would one day sit like a queen on some part of Waitemata's isthmus shores we both implicitly believed, and this belief had taken a turn which shaped our future lives.

Loitering up and down Herekino beach we had already found to be very hard work indeed, and we were yearning for something to do—for anything, in fact, that would hold out the hope of a profitable result. Paying a few dollars a week for a bunk in the Herekino barrack-room and a seat at the *table d'hôte* was of course not a very heavy pecuniary infliction, but having nothing to do but lounge about Herekino had become simply intolerable, and had caused us to exercise our wits as to how we could exchange such a life for something better. We wanted to kill time somehow or other until Government fixed where the capital of the colony was to be, as we fully intended to be purchasers at the first town sale wherever and whenever it came off. We had first thought of exchanging Herekino for Orakei, and asking old Kawau if he would take us in and do for us at his village, but that would only have been exchanging one lounging idleness for another, and, morever, we could do nothing there any more than at Herekino which would in any way benefit us hereafter. But if we could purchase a little spot of our own where we could even grow our own potatoes, *that* would be a step in the right direction, and it would be a home of our own—that *ultima Thule* of every human being save a wandering Arab, and even *he* claims his tent as that.

We remembered how we had seen from our camping-ground at the headland the little island lying in the morning sunlight when we rose, and, opening the tent, looked forth. And we had more than once remarked what a nice little home of our own that island would make until we invested in lots in the captial to be, and settled down for good and all.

On it we could always grow cabbages, provided we could procure the seed from which to raise them. I firmly believe we could not have procured an ounce of cabbage seed for love or money; but at all events we could grow our own potatoes, and if the worst came to the worst we could dig up our own fern-root, for that *dernier ressort* would be duly forthcoming, thanks to a most bountiful Nature. Food for the trouble of digging it, and an inexhaustible supply—think of that!

So we took his majesty the King of Waiau into our confidence, for we well knew that unless he deigned to take us by the hand any efforts of our own would be fruitless. And his Majesty concluded that our little project would not in any way interfere with him, and took us in hand accordingly. He had a soul above wishing to pocket our paltry six dollars a week—in fact, now that the shoal of Sydney landsharks had cleared out, good, kind-hearted Wepiha would have been very glad to have given us the run of our *teeth* for the sake of our tongues, and for our company to beguile his evenings; for, after all, Madame Wepiha was not quite the intellectual fall-back-upon to satisfy him. He did not now require a sleeping dictionary to learn Maori from.

Notwithstanding Wepiha's great knowledge of all the native tribes within three days' travelling distance of his kingdom, it gave him not a little trouble to find out the owners of that little island. One reason was that he made inquiries of the tribes who lived nearest to it, whereas it turned out that the owners were really quite near his own door—only a few miles from Waiau up the Hauraki coast—and at whose settlement he actually had a Pakeha at work building him a boat. And it proved that the owners of that little island were quite willing to part with it; it was a long way from where they lived, and they did not own another acre near it; it was an outlying possession which ran the chance of being seized upon by tribes living near at hand, nor did the owners ever use it in any way: they were only too glad to have the chance of selling it. Such was Wepiha's report to us the first time after he had conferred with the native owners when he went to see how his boat was getting on.

And so it came about one day in the merry month of May, 1840, at a Maori village called Waiomu, on the shore of Te Hauraki, that the chief of the Ngati Tamatera, Te Kanini, and the sub-chiefs Katikati and Ngatai affixed their signatures, not a +, not their marks, but wrote their own signatures to a deed of sale by which that little island in the waters of the Waitemata passed into Pakeha possession. And during the forty years from that long-ago day to this day there has never been a question as to who were the rightful owners of that island, nor a demand made beyond the original price.

I survive, but the three signatories to that deed have all been gathered to their last home, and I can only hope their Maori paradise has received them, and that now they eat *kumara* to their hearts' desire, and can forever smoke the dearly-loved pipe.

From Wepiha we wanted one more good office of friendship, one he was unable to grant, but he did the next best thing he could for us.

We had bought an island, but how could we get to it, or how, having once got to it, could we get away from it, without a boat? But a boat Wepiha could not spare us, neither then nor in the future, for he required the one he was having built at Waiomu for his own use. But he said, when that boat was finished then he would get the Pakeha to build one for us, and he suggested we should proceed to the spot ourselves to help on the work.

We had no choice, and very heartily entered into the proposal, for it would relieve us from loafing about on Herekino beach, it would give us something to do, and, last but not least, it would afford us an admirable opportunity of becoming acquainted with the Maori character, as we should be living for a time in a native settlement, and we should have the Pakeha who was there to act as interpreter.

And so I have arrived at the time when 'we twa' last relics of the once grandly numerous *table d'hôte* were about to leave the King of Waiau to reign once more alone in what glory he might, for Herekino's beach was deserted when we quietly prepared to quit the scene.

The time had been when the departure of grand land-purchasing expeditions caused excitement to prevail from one end to the other of the little bay. But these days were now gone for evermore: the axe had been laid at the root of the King of Waiau's power, for no one required now to propitiate his goodwill and crave his assent before going forth in the endeavour to extinguish native title. The British Government had stepped in and extinguished all the would-be land purchasers by latitude and longitude by a treaty with the Maoris, and so those landsharks, with their bags of unspent gold, had all beaten a precipitate retreat.

I remember well the calm lovely winter morning (it was always lovely when we started to go anywhere then, because time was of no particular value, and we always waited for a fine day) when under a bright sun and a deep blue sky we pushed off in one of Wepiha's boats from Herekino bound for Waiomu. We had no grand *châteaux en Espagne* on this occasion as we had on the last, when we started with Wepiha to behold the Waite-mata and rear a city on its shores: we had now dropped down to the sober earnestness of actual settling. Grand *table d'hôtes* were a thing of the past, nor were we to know them again for many a long year, and before we should ever know them again we were destined to pass through many severe experiences, the lightest of which was sometimes going dinnerless—of being our own cooks with nothing to cook!

But we did not know that then, or perhaps we should not have been so light-hearted and full of hope on that long-ago bright winter morning. We were imbued with a certain delusion that an early settler's life was sur-rounded by a halo of romance which paled the reality into a pleasant episode.

And truly when undertaken in manhood's early years, with a spirit of contended determination to work your way as best you can, and with a certain faith in your power to conquer difficulties, the early settler's life is one, if fortune has been kind to you, which does bear much fruit of romance in after years, though the reality which you pass through meanwhile may seem to be a period savouring only of sternest work.

But when the prize is gained those early trials are remembered, as it were, gratefully. Time has blunted and worn away their sharp edges, and the remembrance of their hardship gives a feeling akin to happiness instead of recalling painful difficulties, for you feel you have fought the good fight, done battle with the world, and have had your reward.

But those only, who have so fought and gained the vic-tory, can enter into and understand the killing despair which falls upon those who have also fought, but, alas! have had no reward.

CHAPTER II

We are Adopted by the Ngati Tamatera

BIG bluff Wepiha, King of Waiau, but now of no
subjects dependent on his barrack-bunk and *table
d'hôte* six-dollar-a-week hospitality, gave us a kind, hearty
shake of the hand and our boat a vigorous shove into
deep water as we bade him farewell that eventful morning when we started, not only for Waiomu, but in the
race of life, for in reality this was our true starting-point.
We had been hovering about the course, not knowing
exactly for which stake we were going to run, but the
die was cast now. We had the world before us, and we
must make or mar our own fortunes, for on ourselves
only we must depend. It did not seem a very aspiring step
to go and live at a small Maori village and help a Pakeha
carpenter to build us a boat, but here we were, turning
our backs on civilisation, deserting the grand Herekino
promenade with no higher object than first to have a
boat built, and thereafter to go and squat on a little island
utterly beyond the pale of even Pakeha sympathy. However, it was setting our feet on the first round of the
ladder.

'*Haere—haere!*' exclaimed Wepiha as the rowers dipped their oars in the water, and we turned our backs
upon the glories of Herekino. There stood the king all
alone. How changed the scene from what it was when I
first landed and saw a knot of gay young fellows playing
pitch-and-toss with sovereigns! Those coins were not so

plentiful again for many a long year, though, fortunately, we did not know it.

'You'll come back here when the boat is finished before you go to the Waitemata', shouted Wepiha to us.

We waved our assent, turned the point of the bay, and were out of sight.

Many were the occasions upon which afterwards for a decade of years I stumbled across Wepiha, but from that day when we left him standing on the shore of his deserted kingdom, his former glory, which had now so completely waned, never returned, and the King of Waiau, by slow but inevitable degrees, was robbed of his once supreme power.

For the influx of Pakehas, consequent upon the colonisation of Maoridom, killed his monopoly with the aborigines. He was elbowed on all sides, but he strongly held his own for a good long time through his early knowledge of the natives and their language.

When the Californian diggings were discovered in after-years, he, with many others, sailed for the Golden Gate, and Poenamo has known him no more.

Kindly are the recollections I have of him, though some avowed he had just that little 'dash of unscrupulousness without which no man can be great' which General Miles McLasky declared to Pio Nono that he flattered himself *he* possessed when offering to take command of the Fenian Army.

The day smiled brightly upon us as we pulled along the shore, shaping our course for Waiomu. There was hardly a breath of wind, though few are the days on Poenamo's shores that there is not a breeze of some kind, which in summer is especially grateful, tempering the warmth so that you repine not at the sunshine, nor growl fiercely at it as they do in Australia. The bright sunshiny winter days, when there is a calm, are feast-days of physical enjoyment, and to those to whom it is given to enjoy a mental feast in gazing on the beauties of Nature those days live in the memory forever.

Even now I can recall the delight of that long-ago day. As we closely skirted the shore, every little bay displayed to us its own peculiar beauty. A bright white shelly beach here, a rich chocolate colour there, one point crowned with overhanging *pohutukawa* trees; from another would rise the brilliant green of the *karaka,* no naked deciduous trees anywhere, but a rich and varied foliage from water's edge to mountain summit, where the grand spreading tops of the *kauri* could be distinguished surmounting every other tree, and proclaiming itself the king of the forest.

The shore in those days was well studded with native villages, and the cultivation around them bespoke an industrious people.

There was a stimulus to their industry at this epoch of their history, for they were labouring under the *tupara* fever. The percussion-gun had made its appearance, and the natives were not slow to see how much more effectual a weapon it was than the old flint brown-bess. And when they saw the *tupara,* the double-barrel gun, the rage at once set in to possess it. They still feared warlike inroads from hostile tribes, and to be able to deliver two shots for one, spoke home to their warlike understandings without any Pakeha persuasion in trading with them. They only did then what we are doing now, for the great tribes of Europe must ever replace the Henry of yesterday by the Martini-Henry of to-day, and by something more quickly and deadly efficient to-morrow.

The Maoris planted great fields of maize and potatoes, and sold the product to Wepiha to provide themselves with *tupara* and gunpowder. It is to be regretted that in the present day the sale of their lands, and the money thus acquired, have converted an industrious into an idle people. Wepiha sent away shiploads and shiploads of produce to the Australian markets, but shipments to foreign ports would not now be necessary, for European local consumption would absorb all. How I should rejoice to see the Maori of to-day the same tiller of the soil he was in the days of which I write! Alas! lords of the soil, they now sell it instead, and idleness doth beget bad habits, and the race deteriorates and dwindles away.

On that long-ago morning we could see them at work in their fields, and as the crew of our boat sang at their oars—the song proclaiming how two Rangatira Pakehas were on their way to Waiomu—they would cease working, and for a minute or two groups would cluster on the shore and send us on our way with the 'Haere—haere' greeting—the salutation of their good wishes.

We were to be landed at our destination by the Pakeha trader who was being sent by Wepiha to Kauwaeranga, one of Wepiha's trading stations, a name now known to civilized ears, though then only known as a native settlement far away up at the source of the Waihou River. Kauwaeranga was a long way off then; it is not any nearer now in distance, but facility of communication brings it so much nearer in time that we smile as we now, in a few hours, arrive at a place that took a long laborious day's travel to reach in those primitive bygone days.

Pulling against wind and tide in an open boat is one thing, steaming along at eight or nine knots an hour is quite another thing. I little thought then that I should live to see daily steamers crossing the Hauraki Gulf at more points than one. Passenger-laden steamers larger than petty ferry-boats were then almost an unknown quantity in Australian waters, quite unknown in Poenamo.

Over the whole expanse of the Hauraki on that morning we saw never a sign of life on its broad waters—no white sails, far less black smoke, far or near. Our own boat summed up and represented the whole existent traffic!

And now as we neared our destination the rowers improvised their boat-song in a louder strain; the words, of course, suited the occasion, and warned the Ngati Tamatera of our approach. It was not long before we could see them beginning to assemble on the beach, for we had heard them pass the cry along, *'Kua tae mai nga Pakeha'* —'The white men have come'—which went echoing up the little valley, and we soon saw a steady stream of all ages and sexes pour down towards the landing-place, at the mouth of a little fresh-water creek.

Assembled on the bank of the stream, there came to us the accustomed *Haere mai! Haere mai!* welcome, with the waving of their mats and blankets. As our boat came within a short distance of the landing-place the shouts of welcome died away. The principal chiefs then retired a little to the back, and squatted down, according to their manner and custom, to receive the visitors, who are expected to walk up to where the chiefs are sitting and commence nose-rubbing.

The excitement consequent upon our arrival, which extended through the whole tribe, was not simply because two Pakehas had arrived, but because they were two Rangatira Pakehas who had come to live amongst them. The ordinary Pakehas the natives had hitherto come in contact with had been for the most part runaway sailors —indeed, not a few were runaway convicts from Australian shores, and they were all addicted to the vice of intemperance. Now, at the time of which I write the natives had an abhorrence of that vice, and continued to have for many a long year—indeed, I lived to see more than a score pass away before I ever saw the spectacle of a native in a state of intoxication. At this time the Maoris were eager to have a Pakeha to come and live at their settlements, as there was the hope he would have a *whare hoko,* and purchase their surplus produce, then they would get the coveted supplies of native trade, which meant in an especial manner percussion-pieces, gunpowder, tobacco, and blankets. When at Herekino we had often heard the chiefs from distant places asking the King of Waiau to confer on them this great boon of a resident Pakeha and a *whare hoko,* but the ever-accompanying stipulation was that he must not be a *tangata riri*

—a man of bad temper—or fond of *waipiro*—stinking-water—*alias* spirits! Such was the term into which they translated rum, which was the prevailing article consumed.

Well, the arrival at Waiomu was not the arrival of Pakehas tainted with convictism or ship-runaway-ism, *waipiro*-ism, or any other *tauretareka*-ism, this last word meaning a slave or low-born, but the two Pakehas who had come to live with them were Rangatiras.

And thus it had come about that the Ngati Tamatera had mustered *en masse* to give us a welcome.

The bow of the boat had no sooner touched the beach than a rush of naked men was made on each side, and, seizing the gunwale, they ran the boat up high and dry before we knew where we were.

It would not have been at all an imposing landing had we come on shore astride on a Maori's back, but now we stepped in a dignified manner on to the beach and walked up to the spot where we saw old Kanini, Katikati, Ngatai, and the other bigwigs of the tribe squatted, folded in their best blankets, waiting to receive us, and repeating in subdued tones as we appeared, '*Haere mai!*'

Had we been Maoris of course we should there and then have also squatted down and rubbed noses. Hereafter I will explain why at such meetings the natives do not jump up and say how glad they are to see you, but welcome you in woe-begone '*Haere mai's',* squatting down and rubbing the lugubrious nose until the spectacle is anything but pleasant to look at.

On the present occasion this custom was not inflicted upon us—so much more pleasant in the breach than in the observance—and Pakeha hand-shaking was the order of the day.

This ceremony was performed with dignified composure by the chiefs; but anon dignity took to flight, for here was a whole tribe who had never yet shaken a Rangatira Pakeha's hand—here was chance which was not to be thrown away.

As we stood beside old Kanini a perfect rush was made to experience in a practical manner the difference between rubbing the lugubrious nose of welcome and shaking the right hand of good-fellowship.

But we soon began to think that very possibly it would have been a lesser martyrdom to have done the aboriginal nose-rubbing, as then we could have restricted that ceremony to the chiefs, their wives and pretty daughters.

Help, however, came to us at last by a sense of the ridiculous seizing the unshaken remainder of the tribe, who tacitly concluded that their Pakehas had behaved like true Rangatiras, and forbore inflicting further handshaking upon them.

And it was thus we made our *entrée* at Waiomu amongst the Ngati Tamatera, and were dubbed their two Rangatira Pakehas, the news thereof speedily spreading among the villages from one end of the Hauraki shore to the other.

CHAPTER III

We Secure Apartments for the Winter Season

THE ceremony concluded of being taken by the hand and heartily shaken into the tribal fraternity of the Ngati Tamatera, we at once set to to look about us for a pleasant spot upon which to pitch the comfortable little tent which, like its owner, was now going to see downright actual service.

As we were arranging *our* household gods, and before we had achieved much in this direction, we were waited upon by old Kanini, who came to present us with one of *his*—in the female form of one of his slave-wives—for I must here proclaim the fact that this new Maori king to whom we had transferred our allegiance was addicted to polygamy.

We did not quarrel with our Solomon of a chief, for in savage communities there be many reasons why a chief should have more than one helpmate, and on this occasion the transferring of one of them to us, set us up with a most respectable matronly attendant and cook. Her duties were solely connected with the culinary department of our establishment, and thus saved us the ignominious work of lighting fires and doing our own cooking! We could hardly have remained *Rangatira* Pakehas had we done so, so of course we should have had to engage a hewer of wood and drawer of water and lighter of cooking fires.

We were thus, comparatively speaking, in domestic clover, Maori clover though it was, but the time was not far off when we were to fall away from such pleasant pastures, and when we should have no chief's slave-wife or any other wife or maid-of-all-work, or anyone to do anything for us. We had commenced our downward course in the social scale of civilisation, and were gaining some knowledge of what was before us. We might dream about the past glories of the *table d'hôte,* but at Herekino it was never seen again, and many a year was to pass away before we were to see anything like it elsewhere.

Our first afternoon among the Ngati Tamatera was spent, as I have said, in putting our new home in order. It was spent by our new friends in sitting in groups watching our proceedings and offering help, their bright, good-natured faces smiling approvingly upon us. A mountainous heap of freshly-gathered fern, half-filling the tent, was presented to us, so we were able to floor it comfortably and make up our soft luxurious beds *à la* Cook with a double allowance.

It was not until we fastened up the tent-door for the night, and prepared to court sleep on our springy fern mattresses, that the natives took themselves off to their own huts, having no longer the opportunity of sitting and looking at their new Pakehas.

I suppose you have not forgotten that I stated Wepiha had a Pakeha here building a boat for him, and that we had come to get one built. This Pakeha, by name Pama*, of course gave us a hearty welcome on our arrival, and it was arranged we were to have a grand consultation *korero* next morning, having enough on our hands that afternoon in getting the tent in order.

And so the following morning, after Mrs. Kina Kanini had given us our breakfast, we settled down to our *korero* with Pama as to the best programme to be carried out. Our first eye-opener as to what was before us was the intimation from Pama that he had not enough 'sawn stuff' to finish the boat he had in hand, and that

[* Palmer.]

the pair of Pakeha sawyers who had been employed some-where in the neighbourhood by Wepiha had bolted in his debt, and as to any chance of our getting a boat built—well, 'How can a man build a boat unless he has the sawn stuff to make it of?' This was one of those knock-down argu-ments that admit of no debating. The boat to which Wepiha's good intentions were to help us was a boat of the future, and evidently so far into the future that it melted away into an intangible form. But here we were: the winter months were before us. We could not make a settlement on the island until spring, so we must just make the best of it where we were until then. Perhaps 'sawn stuff' could be got somehow or other, and we must risk it. But we did not wish to pass the winter in our tent, not but that it would make a very comfortable little habitation, but we had an eye to the future and wished to save the canvas roof to put over our heads when we took possession of the island, and it might be wanted yet again when we removed from the island to settle wherever the Government might fix the capital. So we propounded this plan to Pama—that we should get the natives to build us a small *raupo whare,* which they could run up easily in a week, and that we should hire a boy as a cook and boy-of-all-work.

For although we had Kanini's favourite slave-wife appointed to attend on us, we could only look upon this as the courtesy attendant upon our welcome to Waiomu, and it would not have been good form to have failed to relieve her at an early time from waiting upon us, and to permit her return to her legitimate polygamic duties in the Kanini harem.

Pama quickly put this plan of ours to the right-about by saying—

'There is my house—twice too large for me. I shall divide off half of it for you, and Mrs. Pama'—only he said 'my ooman'—'will do cooking, and washing, and every-thing for you'.

He there and then appealed to Mrs. Rangi Pama,

squatting at that moment on the ground scraping potatoes with a *pipi*-shell for her Pakeha's dinner. And she
responded to the appeal with good-natured alacrity in
only one word, but given in such a tone that a free translation would have read, 'Won't I just!'

It did not need one moment's consideration as to
whether we should accept that offer or not; it at once
solved the necessity of any house-building and servant-
hiring. We knew we had before us in the future any quantity of work in the shape of foraging and cooking for
ourselves without beginning it sooner than we could help,
and, to tell the truth, we did not care how long it was
postponed. The present arrangement was a very fitting
one, and decidedly a step in the right direction, for it
was making a gradual descent from the luxuries we had
lately been revelling in at Herekino to the inevitable,
primitive state of things which awaited us. For that such
did await us there could be no manner of doubt, both
when we took possession of our island home and when
we became the first settlers at the capital—which was to
be—and became citizens thereof.

We were now learning our lessons in the downward
scale of civilisation, but still in a comfortable manner—at
least we hoped that Mrs. Rangi Pama would make it so,
and with this hope and belief we consigned ourselves to
her tender care, and as she was superintended by Pama
we did not fear the result.

So it was all settled, and that night, when we laid our
heads down to rest on our fern pillows in the little tent,
we were soothed to sleep by the murmuring voices of our
new native friends, who sat in groups not far from our
tents, some chanting, some discussing the great event of
the day in the soft Maori language, Mrs. Rangi having
told them of the new duties which had now devolved
upon her.

We slept the sleep of the innocent with minds at ease
that night, all the more soundly from having made so
satisfactory an arrangement for our sojourn at Waiomu.

When we opened the tent-door next morning we looked out upon as lovely a day as ever shone out of the heavens; with the gulf of the Hauraki stretching away before us—away across to the islands where the *Delhi* had lain at anchor—truly a most lovely landscape. Nature seemed asking us to fall in love with our new home among the Maoris, and Nature also invited us, through the medium of the rivulet close at hand, to a morning bath.

Fortunately the rivulet was at hand—it was more than Mrs. Pama was, with any other means of ablution for us. Her establishment did not boast of crockery—she did not possess one atom of it—a wash-hand-basin her eyes had never beheld, but she had an American ship's bucket, and that she offered us. But Nature's offering, in shape of the clear stream at hand, carried the day. It came down from the mountain range away at the back, emptying itself into the Hauraki, a stone's throw from the tent. Improvising a capacious basin in its pebbly channel was only the work of a few minutes; we turned on the tap, and the supply flowed to our hearts' content.

. Our morning toilet was watched with infinite curiosity by a long line of figures of all ages squatting on the top of the bank, my own fair skin and complexion being commented upon in contrast with that of my dark and swarthy companion. I have no doubt, if one could only have heard and understood all the remarks that were made, many a good gastronomic joke was passed of what a dainty morsel my nice white legs would have made had they only been properly cooked.

But our ignorance of Maori kept us in blissful ignorance of after what manner we should have eaten best. I well remember the famous bath we had, and how often in after-years, when the capital *was* a fact, I have longed for the Waiomu water supply—the clear, cool, beautiful water. Delicious was the supply, nor did it matter how many thousand gallons you used, nor were you rated for it; the turncock away up in the mountains never turned off the supply, his reservoir never ran dry, was ever full and ever self-acting.

'*Kua pau te buraguishe*'* came from Rangi's tattooed lips just as we had finished our toilet in the tent, and as she caught sight of us.

' "Breakfast is ready", is it? And so am I, and won't I just walk into it, that's all; you see if I don't; hope the *goahore* is full to the top, for I think I'll play a good figure in seeing to the bottom of it.' All which remarks were utterly thrown away upon Rangi, for she was as steeped in ignorance of the English language as I was of the Maori. I did know that '*kua pau*' meant 'ready', and also 'finished', and '*buraguishe*' was the nearest approach to the pronunciation of our word 'breakfast' of which the native mouth was capable.

Of course our breakfast was the proverbial pork and potatoes—a fare which I can assure modern epicures was anything but to be despised. For the pork of those days was not as these days, for it was Maori-fed—in other words, the pigs were free to roam and get fat how and where they could, or remain lean. In fact they were never too fat, and living for the most part on fern-root, and picking up some maize about the settlements, they were thus clean eaters, and their flesh was firm, not in the least highly flavoured, and therefore did not pall upon the appetite. Moreover, as our fare was almost always corned pork, in this state it had a certain zest which prevented our getting tired of it. Fresh pork, not only every day but three times a day, would soon have become intolerable.

Rangi's resources, however, extended beyond the mere potato accompaniment, for she managed to give a fair *quantum* of the delicious Maori *kumara* and *taro* and cobs of maize, and always a pannikin of tea.

Our plates were made of 'sawn stuff', a square of thin board; our knives were our own clasp-knives; our forks

[* *Parakuihi* would be a closer transliteration of the Maori attempt to say 'breakfast'.]

were our own fingers, or the prong of a shrub, at dis-
cretion; our teacups, of course, were pannikins, obliging
us to have the beverage which was put into them poured
out at the commencement of each meal, which necessity
any new chum will soon learn, should he attempt to put
the hot tin to his lips before the tea has cooled down.

That first Waiomu breakfast was despatched with as
great a gusto as every other one which followed. We
never pined for anything which we saw and could not
get, for nothing else was to be had, and good health
bringing good appetite and never-failing good digestion,
we grew fat upon it. Of course it was a great descent
from the *recherché* dishes of Herekino—*e.g.,* boiled leg
of mutton and caper-sauce; but, as I have stated, it was all
training in the right direction—to that extreme simplicity
of fare which hereafter awaited us. Yes, we lived to covet
Rangi's modest dishes, and to look back upon them with
quite a regretful remembrance.

Few preparations were requisite on Pama's part before
he gave us over half his *whare*; a native was cutting the
poles and another the *raupo* with which the dividing partition was to be constructed, and we also went to work
with practical alacrity, for Pama's being unfurnished
apartments we had forthwith to commence converting
them into furnished ones.

Naturally the first investment took the shape of a
couple of bedsteads and beds. Fresh fern, cut every night,
two feet thick, and spread in springy, luxurious layers,
was a luxury which was all very well when you struck
your tent every morning and left these mountains of
fern behind you, but such luxury was utterly incom-
patible with—'apartments'. There was no help for it; we
had to forego all such luxurious modes of sleeping, and
just rough it like our neighbours in—four-post bedsteads!

The upholsterer's premises—wholesale ones—were
close at hand, at which we could lay in everything that
we required, and we started for them, not with purses
but hatchets in hand. The wholesale supplies we found

represented only the raw materials; it was left to us to manufacture them into fitting shape.

We improvised a most comfortable four-poster after this simple fashion. A few saplings, the thickness of one's wrist, the forest supplied us with almost on entering it; and with some forty or fifty feet of supple-jack. This creeper is of the thickness of your finger, and runs along the ground and goes up the trees and springs across from one tree to the other, spanning great gaps in some mysterious manner of its own—a tough, rascally creeper that won't break, that you can't twist in two, that you must cut, that trips you by the foot or the leg, and sometimes catches you by the neck, the most temper-provoking and the most anathema-producing thing that ever tried the temper of a bush traveller, but so useful withal in its proper places. Well, with our saplings, a coil of supple-jack, and when we got clear of the forest some leaves of the flax-bush, we were already armed with all the raw materials necessary. We took a liberty with Pama's apartments, but one which would hardly give him a claim for damages when we left. Sharpening the saplings for the posts of our bed, we just drove them into the floor—mother earth—at the places we chose, each according to his fancy where his bed should be, then side and end pieces were notched and fitted into each other, and tied with strips of flax-leaf; then we interlaced the supple-jack with the flax-leaf for sacking, making the strong supple-jack go the long way of the bed, and the flax-leaf the cross way. In this simple manner we made a sort of hammock, resembling a net one—one in which after rolling yourself in your blanket, horse-rug, or Maori mat, you could sleep most comfortably. But we were in luxuries' way, for we both had our little shipboard bunk-mattresses, and these were put on our four-posters, and I pity anyone who could not sleep on such a bed, even without the help previously of a hard day's work.

Our bedsteads finished we soon made a table—four posts again—down into the ground, a couple of cross-pieces and some boards on the top, and the thing was done.

Wonderful are the facilities for getting up furnished apartments on good substantial principles when the furniture is not required to stand on a wooden floor. Quickness of construction and a permanent solidity arise out of an earthen one, unattainable through any other means. No one ever furnished their apartments more regardless of expense than we did ours. Our chief did not even ask us for a single copper—*i.e.,* as much tobacco as would fill his pipe, which would have represented a copper coin—for our raw materials, so no wonder we went ahead in the furnishing line!

Before the week was over we had positively elevated ourselves to three-legged stools; but I am bound to confess, in strict honesty, that as these were *not* fixtures, and consequently portable, they were most undoubtedly shaky! Our beds we jumped into in the most defiant and reckless manner, with the conscious feeling that they were equal to the occasion. But these three-legged stools were a caution, and created a habit of approaching them and putting them to their intended use in a wary manner, which stuck to us when the time came that we *had* chairs to sit upon, and suggested the idea to outsiders that we were afraid of concealed needles and pins, and consequently came to an anchor cautiously.

CHAPTER IV

De Pluribus Maori Rebus

IF I am to be a true chronicler of the times of which I write, it devolves upon me to narrate the ways in which some of the pioneer Pakehas took the aborigines by the hand and guided them into civilisation.

Some of these ways, it is true, were not according to a strictly moral interpretation of what civilisation ought to be, but great allowances must be made, and it behoves us in these later days, when the equality of the sexes is an accomplished fact, not to sit in judgment too severely over a backsliding into some native customs at a time when Maori manners only prevailed.

If one step back was taken, there still remained a credit balance to the two steps forward, and then there were those who never took the step to the rear; so, on the whole, some virtue did prevail, though no cakes or ale were to the fore.

When the old Kanini heard of our arrangement with Pama, and that we were to be taken in and cared for after the manner I have narrated, a great load of anxiety was lifted off the old man's mind. The fact was, he had been casting about to find out from what source he could supply his newly-acquired Pakehas with temporary wives. You see, if we had chosen to forget the godly ways in which our youth had been reared, and had elected to run riot in these Polynesian ways of securing domestic drudges, young chieftainesses would not have been wanting to adorn our *raupo whare* hearths. Great was the relief, therefore, to old Kanini when he learnt from Pama that we did not expect to be provided with the customary female helpmates.

But I regret to have to state the fact that the relief thus afforded to the old chief did not arise from any gratification at the moral course pursued by his Pakeha, but simply because his own only daughter, being still under her teens, was not available, and that it so happened there were no other young chieftainesses in the tribe who were in the market; and, finally, it would have been quite a severe blow had he been compelled to go and borrow two young ladies from any other sub-tribe, for then the two Rangatira Pakeha would not have belonged wholly and solely to himself, but would have been at least one-half the property of the tribe which had furnished the Pakehas with their 'better halves'.

This may appear a very sad revelation, but the old Kanini was none the less a good and a moral man—after the light in which it had pleased Providence he should be brought up. Plurality of wives is a very ancient institution, as all good Christians who read their Bibles know. Kanini could not hold a candle to old Solomon in this direction, but in good sound sense I should not have minded backing him, for Kanini was a man of no ordinary intellect and ability.

Then again, as to the custom of the chiefs giving wives to all the Pakehas who came to live at their settlements, there was sound moral philosophy at the bottom of it, as, indeed, there was to be found in almost all their manners and customs, however peculiar these might appear at first sight to the uninitiated. The foible of eating each other, if not to be explained on philosophical principles, might be palliated on human nature wants, and as there were no animals upon which they could prey when the craving to eat flesh overcame them, they could not help themselves but by helping themselves—to themselves! But I have digressed from the explanation I had in hand regarding the philosophy of giving wives to all Pakehas, and it was this: Human nature being human nature, and it being found rather impossible to convert it into anything resembling Divine nature, it had to be dealt with accordingly. 'We will give the Pakeha a wife of his own, and then he will have no excuse for carrying on any flirtations with ours.' Of course if any such flirtations assumed serious proportions the Divorce Court proceedings took a very summary form—the chief might have forgiven, but more probably would have tomahawked, his erring squaw, and, performing the latter process on the Pakeha, would thereafter have eaten him. But as it did not now pay to eat useful Pakehas, who supplied them with guns and powder, pipes and tobacco, it better preserved all things, and especially the moral proprieties, to supply the Pakeha with wives, and keep him alive. In this form in their midst he was good to sponge upon for a *'puru'** at any hour of the day, but when killed and eaten could only be a pleasing remembrance of a past gratification!

But Tangata Maori being essentially a hard, practical, matter-of-fact animal, shaped his conduct to attain the greatest possible gain at smallest possible cost, and thus it came about that young chieftainesses were a cheap bait with which to lure and secure the Pakeha.

Our first week at Waiomu was not altogether uneventful and not altogether pleasant, as we had our patience tried to its uttermost in rather a peculiar manner. That fact that Kanini had bagged a brace of Rangatira Pakehas became known from one end of the Hauraki to the other in just about as short a time as if there had been telegraph stations the whole way. The result was that a stream of visitors set in in a strong current to rub noses with the old man—ostensibly to do this, but in reality to satiate their curiosity in having a look at us and hearing all about us, and to whom we were to be married was, of course, a point of intense interest.

* *Puru*, as much tobacco as would fill a pipe.

Now every time any of these visitors came we had no choice but to gratify their curiosity by turning out for inspection. But inasmuch as we only knew Maori enough to the extent of being able to say, *'Tena koe?'* ('How do you do?'), and as that terminated our conversational powers in their vernacular, nothing then was left us but to stare at each other. In this little part of the performance we had no chance against our new friends, who beat us hollow at it. Sitting squatted on the ground, rolled up in their mats, or last new blanket donned for the occasion, they had a power of endurance which put to shame us poor civilized creatures.

It was the same scene over again as that at the Debtor's Prison so graphically described in *Pickwick,* where all the turnkeys stood round the newly incarcerated to take his likeness, staring until the physiognomy was indelibly stamped on their memories. I am certain the numbers that learnt us by heart, and the persevering manner in which our likenesses were taken, made it a moral impossibility that either of us could ever do an *incognito* excursion on the shores of the Hauraki.

We grew wiser the next day, and dodged the infliction by changing the venue to the shed where Pama was working at the boat, and pressing his services into use as interpreter we held conversations with our many visitors. In these conversations we endeavoured to impress the native mind with our superiority in the scale of human civilisation by the deep and searching questions we put regarding their own manners and customs compared with our own, as laid down to them in what we considered convincingly lucid language. But I am free to confess that when they took their departure we felt very doubtful as to the impression we had made, and we had rather a disappointing conviction when these parleys ended, and when, on the visitors leaving, Pama distributed a *puru* amongst the more distinguished and enlightened, that Pama was high in the scale of Maori estimation as compared to us, Rangatira though we were!

The incessant cooking of food which went on to administer the customary hospitality to all these strangers was something terrible, and the way in which the provisions were punished was something to remember and was a heavy strain on the Ngati Tamatera commissariat. The tribe was paying the penalty, and a pretty smart one, for having the high privilege of possessing show Pakehas.

A week pretty nearly exhausted the supply of visitors, and we felt we were now at liberty to absent ourselves, as we could do so without wounding the feelings of 'our tribe', who would not have been pleased had we not been forthcoming to be exhibited.

With the second week we had to face the question of what we were to do and how we were to occupy ourselves under the disheartening circumstances in which we were placed by Pama's inability to build us a boat from want of material. We were on the horns of a dilemma, for it was patent that it was impossible to go and take possession of our island unless we had some means of transit. True, we might get some chance of being taken and landed on it, but then we should be prisoners, and might starve for want of any other food save fern-root; but if we had even a canoe we might, when hard up, paddle up to Orakei and get a kit of potatoes. Even sulky Te Hira would not grudge us that, in return, of course, for a fig of tobacco.

But on appealing to old Kanini to spare us a canoe, he said he had none, and we were beginning to feel rather queer over our position, when Pama, inspired by a bright idea, came to the rescue and solved the difficulty:

'There is a grand large *kauri* tree—lying felled near the edge of the forest ridge—would make a splendid canoe, though a little heavy to paddle up. Why not turn to and dig it out? Old man will sell you the tree for a couple of dollars!'

A happy thought and one which was adopted on the spot; old Kanini was only too glad to sell us the *kauri* tree; and the promised occupation chimed in with our

views in every way. We wanted to kill time and get
through the winter months before going to live on our
island, and we wanted by living amongst the natives to
get an insight into their character, and manners, and
customs.

For it was very evident that our future in the land
could not be disconnected with the dominant race, and
it was equally evident that the Maori would remain the
dominant race for a great many years.

It would, therefore, be good sound policy to acquire
any knowledge which might enable us to cultivate
friendly relations with the Maoris, who would inevitably
remain a prominent factor in the future history of the
colony for a good many years to come.

By cultivating friendly relations with the Ngati Tamatera, and through them coming in contact with other
tribes, we hoped to become favourably known on the
shores of the Hauraki; and should the future, unhappily,
foment squabbles between the two races, the time might
come when we should be glad to shelter ourselves under
the *mana* (the protection) of good old Kanini. As yet we
were steeped in ignorance of native character. We only
knew that the race seemed one endowed with marvellous
equanimity of temper, and with a keen perception of the
advantage of looking after number one. Of the inner and
deeper mind, of the motives which might lead to political
action, we knew nothing; these had all to be discovered,
and we would fain read and understand these pages of
Maori character.

We were fortunately circumstanced, as it turned out,
for doing this, for it soon became impressed upon us that
Kanini was a man of no ordinary intellect, and in Pama,
who would be our interpreter, we had a man who,
though somewhat uneducated, had all his wits about him
and great reasoning powers withal.

The *kauri* tree was bought. Pama furnished us with
squaring-axes, and so it fell out that just as the last of the
visitors to whom we had to sit for our likenesses had left,

we had all our preparations completed for commencing our canoe-digging.

And one glorious morning, Rangi having given us an early pot of pork and potatoes and primed us with a small kit of boiled *kumara* for a midday cold collation, we sallied forth from Pama's *whare,* axes on shoulder, to commence our Robinson Crusoe work.

That bright, glorious, sunny winter morning was the 14th day of June, 1840!

CHAPTER V

A Maori Wake

S OME three weeks had elapsed since we had taken up
our abode at Waiomu, and the end of a beautiful
autumn had been followed by the commencement of a
mild and lovely winter.

We had been busy every day for a fortnight in the
forest, hewing the sides of the huge pine tree, which now
began to assume somewhat of its intended shape and
form, when one forenoon, as we were hard at work, we
were startled to hear rising from the valley beneath, the
loud long wailing death-cry.

Throwing down our axes we went to the edge of the
forest, from whence we could look down upon the whole
valley and the village, but before we reached it the report
from many muskets began to sound from the village,
and soon spread up the whole valley.

On gaining the edge of the forest we could see the
Maoris hastening from all quarters towards one particular spot. We at once knew what had happened, for we
recognised the spot as where young Ngatai's *whare* was,
and we were aware he was in the last stage of consumption. Death had visited a Ngati Tamatera chief, and the
wail was taken up at each scattered hut along the valley
until it sounded faintly and mournfully on the ear from
the far distance. I had always brought a gun with me, bor-
rowed from Pama, in the hope of being able to cater for

Mrs. Pama's *cuisine* by bringing home a brace or two of *kukupa,* so, hastening back for it, I returned again to the edge of the forest, and fired a number of minute-guns to show our Maori friends that their Pakehas sympathised with them in their bereavement. This duty performed we returned to our work, and continued at it until sunset.

All day we heard the death-wail, and we could distinguish that the musketry reports became more and more concentrated towards one point—Ngatai's house.

The sun was sinking behind the Wairoa ranges when we descended into the valley from our work, and we were greeted with the same news on all sides—'*Kua mate a Ngatai*'. We knew of course he was dead, and as we neared his hut the death-wail and musket-firing became louder and louder; and at last, as we arrived at the spot, we saw quite a large assemblage of natives standing in a semi-circle in front of the hut going through their accepted and customary rites on such occasions.

The Ngati Tamatera having many near neighbours up and down the shores of the Hauraki, we could see that not a few strangers had already arrived to pay the visit of ceremony in honour of the dead, and in compliment to the living, of the tribe, and, if the truth must be told, with the due appreciation of the usual attendant feast.

We stopped to look at the ceremony, already in full swing, and I performed my part in proper Maori fashion, by discharging some volleys from my gun.

The particular rites in which we could not, or rather would not, take a part, I must dilate upon shortly. As the performance was of an altogether novel character, I think it worth while to try to describe it so that you may have the strange picture before you. As this picture, however, will contain portions not altogether pleasant to look upon, I give fair warning, so that if you happen to be in a squeamish mood the next page or two had better be skipped. As I am not inventing, but simply narrating facts, I absolve myself from all responsibility if you elect to *read* what we *saw*.

I have already stated that we found the obsequies in full swing, short as had been the time for preparation since the death-wail had startled us at our work that morning in the forest. Poor Ngatai, the youngest of the three chiefs who had signed the deed of sale of the island to us, had indeed passed away to the land of spirits, but there lay before us in state the frail mortal remains that had so lately owned that name.

The body, having the face uncovered, was wrapped up in blankets and native mats, and was laid out a short distance in front of a fence which had already been erected—a sort of small guard-fence, covered with *raupo,* having a back and two ends sloping away at an angle, so that an uninterrupted view might be afforded to the extended semi-circle of mourners in front. On this fence were hung almost the whole of the deceased's personal effects—his blankets, the highly-valued *kaitaka* mat (which has now almost ceased to be made), his musket and double-barrelled gun, cartouche-box, tomahawk, and many other things—all destined to hang there forever, tabooed to the memory of the departed. No sacrilegious hand, however coveted the articles, will ever disturb them. —there they will hang until the fence rots to the ground, if they have not first rotted away and fallen down.

At one side of the body sat old Kanini as chief mourner, muffled up in his flax mat and looking un-utterably woeful.

And little wonder, poor old man, considering what was before him, for he well knew the martrydom he had to go through whilst others only wept—Maori fashion—and feasted.

I shall now endeavour to describe how the mourners went through these respective processes, the first being compulsory before indulging in the last, for no one feasted until first having mourned in the orthodox Maori fashion.

About twenty or thirty yards in front of the fence we saw the semi-circle of mourners—men and women—in all the different stages of the wail in words, and bodily infliction in deeds, as custom dictated, but to understand how some of them had arrived at the very grotesque condition in which we then saw them the only way is to begin with some newly-arrived mourners and watch the process *ab initio*. Late though it was in the evening, a fresh canoe-load had just arrived, so we had an opportunity of witnessing a Maori wake.

Having taken up their position in front of poor dead Ngatai, they stood for a minute or two hanging down their heads, and then the old women of the party broke into a well-sustained hum-m-m, prolonging the -m-through the nose, a perfect imitation of a naughty child trying to get up a cry—just exactly what these old women were aiming at.

The younger of the new mourners had to take much more frequent breath in doing their hums, which they gave out very *sotto voce*, or rather *sotto naso*!

It was perfectly evident how difficult it was for young human nature to do this wailing hum as it ought to be done, and was now being done by the older stagers.

After getting into the full swing of the hum-wail, the next stage was to end this with a short ejaculatory sentence in eulogy of the deceased, and when they reached the grand full swing, the hum through the nose had disappeared, and the true wail-cry was given out loud and strong. When they had exhausted their sentences of eulogy they then fell back upon a more self-scarifying way of proving their grief, as I shall describe now.

But first look at those old women; why they really must have been crying in earnest, as there was proof, for they did not use pocket-handkerchiefs—no, nor their fingers instead either; one wished they would do so to discard that dirty nose-pendant.

What! those old women remove that emblem of grief! The shades of Ngatai forbid! the very thought is sacrilege!

Know that by the length of these nasal pendants was

measured the depth of feeling for the departed. No, not until poor human nature is exhausted and can wail no more, and can increase no more that nasal emblem of great grief and sorrow, shall it be shorn of its woe-cried length!

But what did they do next, these old withered hags, with stooping figures, their hands resting on their knees as they stood, a mat from waist to knee all their attire?

Look! That old hag as she ended her chanting, wailing moan, gave herself a cut down the cheek from the eye to the corner of the mouth: it drew blood! Another wailing moan is followed by another scarification on the opposite cheek, using a sharp-edged shell as the instrument of self-torture.

Look at the old woman next her! She has left nothing more of the face to scarify, and she has now begun the same process on her breast and bosom! And yet another—now past these two stages—has taken to her arms, and lo! still another—past all these three stages, face, bosom, arms—still not content, has begun at her knees, and only rests content on getting to her ankles!

Well tried, young chieftainess! but your novice hand it yet unskilled in these flesh-wounds; wait awhile, and when the freshness and bloom of youth shall have passed away, your hand will be bolder and steadier. To you it is only given as yet to reach a respectably duly mourning face, but be not ashamed, for see, your younger sister has succumbed to a sitting posture, and, unable to keep up even the hum-m-m any longer, is fain to bury her head in her mat and so hide pretended nasal pendants in silence!

The men made but a very sorry figure in these exhibitions. They buried their heads and affected the hum-m-m wail, but they could not keep it up; and as no dignity was to be got out of it, they very soon took refuge in firing salutes from their muskets.

The great chiefs of the different tribes who came to do the visits of mourning seldom took their places in the circle, but went and sat down beside old Kanini and took a fearful spell of the genuine lugubrious nose-rubbing out of the poor old martyr. Squatted on the ground, they would positively keep their noses in strict contact for half-an-hour at a stretch, and keep a gradually-increasing moistening hum-m-m until really they were far from pleasant to look upon. Nasal pendants of the peculiar description engendered by this process did not constitute a thing of beauty.

Some of the very great chiefs, however, were compelled to wipe away, not a tear, but a pendant, and then came forward to deliver a funeral oration. Very graceful was the manner in which this was commenced; most exciting generally was the manner in which it was concluded.

Rising from the old Kanini's side a chief with glistening *kaitaka* mat folded around him like a Roman toga, paces quietly and sedately forward until he reaches the circle of mourners, when he suddenly stops, faces about, and with slightly-quickened step paces back towards Kanini and the body lying in state and delivers a sentence of his oration, arresting his further advance close to the chief. He now again turns round and walks deliberately back in silence to the starting-point of the mourners, when again he suddenly faces Kanini, and, advancing this time more quickly than the last, he delivers another short sentence—never more than eight or ten words. Gradually, as he warms in his theme, he makes his advance and delivers his sentence at an increased rapidity. And soon the dignified toga-draped orator begins to look a little wild; the flax mat now flies loosely about him, for he almost runs forward, and ends with a jump in the air almost at Kanini's feet, and looking rather as if he had intended to go clear over him! But the turning round and pacing back is always most sedately performed to give due breathing and composing time to arrange his next sentence.

Wonderfully strange is the effect that this at last produces when the speaker has worked himself up to the highest stage of intense action, when he rushes forward, his mat flying wildly around him, brandishing with a peculiar quivering motion a *taiaha*—wooden broadsword —or a tomahawk, rushing forward with high-toned voice and hastily-spoken words, ending his advance with a sudden jump in the air, and in a moment assuming the most statuesque repose, and in the most quiet and dignified manner again pacing back.

A hurricane and a calm—most profound calm. But see now he can no longer bear the restraint of his long toga about his body; he has flung it aside; he is no calm, dignified toga-robed orator now, but a savage, nude, save a short mat hanging from waist to knee, which is sometimes conspicuous by its absence, he is all fiery gesticulation, and as he rushes forward he gives his bare leg a great slap with one hand, with the other brandishing his *taiaha* high in air.

At last the hurricane has expended itself, all the warlike deeds and acts of prowess of the dead chief have been held up for emulation, and suddenly changing to the statuesque repose he ends with a dirge chanted in a low monotonous tone. To give some idea of what were the virtues most held in estimation amongst Maoris, the following is a free translation of a dirge chanted over Ngatai:

> Oh! wail for the dead and weep,
> Long, long shall Ngatai sleep;
>   Our friend and chief and brother,
>   The good Ngapora's son,
>   Where shall we find another
>   To rule as he has done?
> Ah! wail for the dead and weep,
> When shall he wake from sleep?
>
> Brave was he in battle-field,
> Dauntless was he, nor known to yield;
> Steady he poised his spear on high,
> `Swift did his deadly weapon fly.

Yet fell he not from *mere** blow,
Alas! he pined and wasted low;
An evil eye wiled him away,
And spellbound, helpless—there he lay.

So gentle was his heart and true,
That all who knew him loved him too;
Fond of his wife, fond of his child,
Not soon provoked, but kind and mild,

Ah! wail for the dead and weep,
His spirit does not sleep,
But o'er us it doth hover,
To hear our every sigh,
And mark how friend and brother
In grief and woe do cry.
Ah! Ngatai, wherefore dost thou sleep,
And leave us here to wail and weep?

After each new arrival had performed the proper amount of ʿtangi-ing wailing at the semi-circle they retired to feast, and to gossip—the latter I believe a greater treat than the former.

The Maori wake in the days of which I write was in every way most decorous; intoxicating liquids never passed the Maoris' lips; there were no toasts to the memory of the deceased, and the health of the living relatives; no draining of inebriating cups at Waiomu.

Cold spring-water left no imbibers prostrate, but if the wake lacked the drinking element, *certes* it did not the eating power, for the quantity of the Ngati Tamatera provisions which were consumed was a caution, and compelled the tribe to fall back upon fern-root before their new crop of potatoes came to their relief in the spring.

You may remember that when I began the description of this funeral we had just returned from our forest work. We stood watching the strange scene until sunset,

* *Mere,* a highly-prized small hand-weapon of war made from greenstone, used in close combat.

when the deepening gloom sent us home to our evening meal of Rangi's preparing.

The good housewife—for such indeed she was to us in her own quiet way—told us how the minute-guns I had fired at the opening of the forest had pleased old Kanini and his people.

During the evening, and now again throughout the night, a sudden burst of the death-wail would break upon the stillness as some old devotee, awakening with the feeling strong upon her that she was still in the funereal harness, would start off quite unrestrainable at the full wailing pace.

Spare yourselves, old women—spare yourselves: much is still in store for you; you have a long, long journey before you reach the last stage of the Ngati Tamatera obsequies, wailing enough you will have—scarifying to your hearts' content. Spare yourselves!

CHAPTER VI

A Gunpowder Explosion : The Doctor Wanted

THE following morning was ushered in with a repetition of the Maori minute-guns; indeed, stray shots and a strong death-wail had been breaking on our ears throughout the night, but with the sun the salute-firing had set in again in full force.

We had just finished our breakfast, and were on the point of starting to our work in the forest, when we heard a tremendous report, far beyond anything any musket could give forth—much more like a cannon. We stood for a moment wondering what could have happened, when two natives, perfectly nude, rushed past where we were standing and precipitated themselves into the rivulet which flowed close past our door; then came rushing after a perfect crowd of natives, howling furiously, in wild despair, the most concentrated, agonising death-wail conceivable!

What had happened? What awful catastrophe had befallen the tribe?

They stood at the river-side rending the air with cries of 'Kua mate te Rite!—kua mate te Pirete!'

What did they mean? In those two chiefs we now recognised the men who had just rushed past us and jumped into a pool in the river—there they were alive fast enough, nothing kua mate dead about them!

They were certainly looking awfully scared, but they

might well be so on being howled over in that fearful way, and told that they were dead!

Had a stranger been present he would have imagined it was a case of evil spirits causing honest people to rush down steep places, for Pama had no sooner found out the reason of all this row than he communicated it to me, and we were seen suddenly rushing into the pool beside the two chiefs. We turned them about and all round, examining their shiny black skins with eager haste, and then we re-consigned them to their self-sought bath, and betook ourselves on to dry land again.

The loud report we had heard was the explosion of some gunpowder; the two chiefs had got burnt by it and had rushed into the river, and as I found the wounds were hardly skin-deep, and extended over a very small surface, I allowed them to indulge in the cold-water cure which they had sought.

The accident had come about in this way: a fresh distribution of powder had to be made to supply the wants of the salute-firers over Ngatai, and it was being served out from an open keg of gunpowder. A slave-boy was sitting on the ground with the keg between his legs doling out the loose powder, and no doubt in a very loose way. The two chiefs (whom I have left in the river all this time) had been adjusting a new flint to one of their old muskets, and must needs try how it acted, but they tried it just a little too close to the open keg of powder, and a spark fell into it—hence the explosion. The result to the slave-boy was that he was about split in two, and killed there and then, the chiefs getting off with a few superficial burns. Of course there was great dread that the two chiefs were done for; as for the slave-boy, the tribe could not spare time to wail over him when they had two big chiefs demanding their sympathies, and Ngatai also in hand.

My little tent was still standing, not having been struck since we moved out of it into Pama's *whare,* so I converted it into an hospital for the two patients, and

being speedily spread with fresh fern and covered with
mats, the chiefs found themselves, within half-an-hour of
the accident, installed in most comfortable, though certainly unexepected, quarters. Their burns were of a
very superficial kind, and only in one or two small
patches, and really required nothing to be done, or I
should not have allowed them to continue their self-
sought cold bath. The application of outward sympathy
was the only salve wanted, and this was being supplied
in such a wholesale manner by all the old women of the
settlement howling in front of the tent-door that 'All
their chiefs would die', and such cheering remarks, that
I came to the conclusion the sooner my patients were
relieved of the doleful row outside the better. Moreover,
we did not want a gang of *tangi*-ing old women quite
so close to our own quarters, so I caused Pama to intimate
in very serious language—translating mine and also the
solemnity of my countenance into his own when deliver-
ing the announcement—that absolute quiet was essential
to the recovery of their chiefs, and that they must do no
tangi-ing nearer than where poor Ngatai lay in state.

This order had the effect of directing back to its original channel the flow of tears which had been diverted
from their legitimate source by the gunpowder explosion.
It is very doubtful, however, if my injunction of quietness
would have been respected but for the fact that the old
women had got poor Ngatai to fall back upon, for being
now so thoroughly up to mourning pitch, they felt they
could suffer and be strong on rather easy conditions to
themselves. However, they betook themselves to their
original occupation in front of Ngatai, and quiet reigned
around the tent and our *whare*—thus two birds were
killed with one stone!

As this catastrophe had so completely broken in upon
our day we did not go to our forest work, but made a
holiday of it, watching all the ceremonies and observances connected with the deceased chief. A continued
stream of arrivals kept pouring in from all quarters, the

semi-circle of mourners was kept well filled, and poor old Kanini had to maintain his post of honour against all comers. His was no sinecure; every arrival brought a given number of chiefs of note, and of such aristocratic standing that they were entitled to the seat of honour beside Kanini and a personal rub of the old man's nose.

Whilst others came and went the old man had to remain like a sentinel beside the corpse—he was the victim upon whom all the strangers of sufficient rank bore down with the inevitable and not-to-be-denied salutation of rubbing the lugubrious nose!

Day after day went by and still new mourners kept dropping in, keeping Kanini to his post. Then, besides, to add to his inflictions, he was *tapu,* and dare not touch food with his own hands. These had become *tapu* from having 'laid out' Ngatai, and an old woman had to come and feed him by putting his food into his mouth! Sometimes she would be behind time—the fact was, every woman in the tribe was kept hard at work from morning until night preparing food for the swarms of mourners, who, like a plague of locusts, threatened to eat everything from off the land owned by the Ngati Tamatera. The old woman, as I was saying, would sometimes be behind time, or poor Kanini's appetite would be in advance of it, and then the old man would have to go down upon his knees, his hands behind his back, as far away as possible from the food, and grub into a kit of provisions more like a pig than anything else, and catch hold of a mouthful the best way he could.

Eventually a sort of provision platform was erected to suit the emergency, so that he could take occasional snatches when hard put to it without having to wait for woman's assistance, or descend, knees to the earth and face to the ground, like a Mussulman saying his prayers.

Perhaps you may be mentally exclaiming, 'And this is the old man you want us to believe to be such a superior savage. "Transplant him to a civilized community and he would do it honour", and all that sort of highflown nonsense! If so, why does he submit to such disgusting and stupid customs? No man of sense would.' This is, perhaps, what you are saying to yourselves.

Listen to me, my children. Are not you in your civilized state the slaves of fashion and of customs as absurd? Of course you are; and *certes,* even in these our days of advanced civilization, an Irish wake would far outdo in stupid and almost gross customs all that I have described as taking place at Waiomu. We may not believe in many of the fashions of the day, but are we not slaves to them?

Kanini did not believe much in *tapu* as I shall hereafter prove to you. He was only, like you, the slave to the opinions and fashions of the society in which he was living. Well! and absurd as many of the fashions of our day are, still there is no use running a tilt against the accepted manners and customs of our day—at least, sensible people don't do it.

And Kanini *was* a sensible man!

I have already stated that his tribe had not embraced Christianity—the missionary had not converted them, or, more properly speaking, he had failed with the old man, for had he turned *mihinare** his tribe would forthwith have followed suit. They were all *tewara,* which is the nearest approach to the word 'devils' in the Maori tongue, which was the complimentary name the enlightened early missionaries gave to all who would not submit to their preachings and accept their dogmas.

Kanini was a *tewara.* The missionary had attempted to storm the *tapu* of the old man, but in vain. He had been driven forth discomfited one day, so Pama told us.

The *mihinare* had been trying to terrify the old chief into a more satisfactory belief by portraying all the terrors of the future punishment that would overtake the unconverted. 'You will be cast forth into outer darkness into a bottomless pit'—the old man had never heard of a pit without a bottom before—'where all such as you are consigned to everlasting punishment amongst howling fiends, to be burnt in brimstone and hell-fire', etc.

[* Campbell spells this word 'meetinary'.]

'*Heoi ano! heoi ano!*' ('Enough! enough!') exclaimed Kanini, 'that won't do. How can there be fire in a place of utter darkness?'

'But my friend Kanini——'

'But me no buts', quoth Kanini, who thought he had found out the converting *mihinare* and bowled him over, by having caught him inventing for the nonce. And so Kanini remained a *tewara,* but for good sound reasons of his own which I shall tell you by-and-by. I think I have already mentioned that the old chief did not much believe in the *tapu,* the miseries of which we saw him so uncomplainingly undergoing. This knowledge of his character came to us at a later period of our sojourn at Waiomu, though I am going to tell you about it now.

Many were the conversations we had during the winter evenings with the old man, getting Pama to act as interpreter; and before our canoe was finished we had gained a pretty clear insight into the native mind and their manners and customs. It was on one of these evenings we asked Kanini why he did not cease to labour under the ignominious epithet of *tewara.* The old man benignly smiled, as who should ask whether being called a devil made or marred any man, and he calmly replied:

'What would you have me do? I am now an old man; why change my religion, or allow my people to change theirs, and so risk my power over my tribe? The *tapu* has served my purpose—will serve for my day. Your religion may be good—may be better—but how know I what my people may learn with it? Perhaps not respect for me and obedience to their chiefs. No, no; the religion of my fathers is good enough for me, good enough for my people, and if they only pray to the evil gods to leave them alone, no fear of the good ones doing them any harm—you don't require to pray to *them.* And when I die', he said, 'my spirit will pass away from Muriwhenua*,

---

* A bold headland on the coast. The Maoris have a tradition that on their death the disembodied spirit wings its flight from off this lofty headland into the world of spirits.

and I shall eat *kumara,* and smoke my pipe I hope, and be happy forever.'

Such was the simple Maori idea of Paradise; its happiness prospectively increased since the advent of Pakeha tobacco!

Yes—a future believed in, and a world of spirits!

'And your spirit, Kanini, what *is* that?'

'The Pakeha asks me, the poor old Kanini, what is a spirit? *Kahore au e matau,* I don't understand. How can I tell? Look!' he said, as the lamplight threw his shadow on the wall, and pointing to his shadow, moving as he moved, he said—

'Look! Can the Pakeha take hold of that?'

Beautifully answered, old man! even if thou art a savage there is poetry in thy nature!

CHAPTER VII

Steeped in Tapu

THE two chiefs who had experimented with the new flint over the keg of gunpowder with so fatal a result to the poor slave-boy, and with so scorching an effect upon themselves, continued in my tent under my medical treatment. As for the slave-boy, he was never mentioned; he had been killed: what of that? Perhaps some old woman did a quiet *tangi* over his grave, but no semi-circle of mourners performed funeral rites over his remains. The poor mangled body had been huddled into a hole anyhow; who could think of him when Ngatai lay in state, and Te Rite and Te Pirete lay burnt in the Pakeha's tent?

Was the poor slave-boy any worse off amongst his fellow savage brethren in this far-off land than the poor —not slave, but free—man amongst *his* civilized fellow-men in the Old Country? Not one whit—I rather imagine infinitely better off. The slave of the Maori was only one in name; he or she of course had to do more work, but generally fared just as well as the master. They did no cruel work, and certainly, as a rule, much less hard work than the labourer at home. The latter had certainly one advantage over the Maori slave, for he was not occasionally cooked and eaten. But then *when* alive the slave had always plenty to eat; he could never starve as the poor at home do. Again, he could always build himself a comfortable *whare*, and of fuel have as much as

he chose to cut and revel in. He thus had good shelter
and warmth and plenty to eat and drink. Happy slave!

What though no one cried over his grave when he
was split in two by the keg of gunpowder, still he was
decently buried, though huddled into mother earth in a
hurry. Not so always the deserted and forsaken poor at
home; sometimes they minister to science on the students'
dissecting-table before the disjointed members are
huddled into a coffin and buried within a given time,
according to Act of Parliament. What is the value of a
life—what the manner of a burial—even according to the
country we live in, and the current of ideas that prevail?
Have I never told you what happened to me once when
driving through a narrow thoroughfare with Captain
—— in his buggy in Calcutta? Suddenly a little child
rushed across the narrow street, and before we could pull
up we were over it. Captain —— was about to stop to see
what had happened, but the syce had no idea of doing
such a thing, and he exclaimed, '*Jeldi jou—jeldi jou*'—
Go on quickly. 'But perhaps we have killed the child.'
'Well, never mind; if they can buy wood to burn it they
will burn it' and if they can't they will put it into the
Ganges.' At the worst the sacred waters of that river
would bear it away as it bears away countless of the poor
who cannot afford cremation!

But I diverge; let me go back to my legitimate narrative. It was ten years later before I visited, as a traveller,
the City of Palaces.

The two chiefs, whose burns, as I have stated, were very
superficial, were getting on famously; they were enjoying
the quiet comfort of the little tent, relieved by judicious
visits of gossiping, not *tangi*-ing, friends, and I fully
expected to dismiss both my patients sound and whole
again before long.

My hopes, however, were doomed to a great disappointment. Native superstition was about to step in and play a
curious drama by laying hold of one of my patients and
making him enact one of the strangest of tragedies.

One morning, before setting out for our daily forest work, and while I was dressing Te Pirete's skin-deep wounds—much more slight than those of his brother chief—I was informed that during the night the spirit of dead Ngatai had appeared to him, upbraiding him for lying in the same tent as Te Rite, who was a so much greater chief, and telling him that he ought to have known it was against all proper *tapu* observances for him to be under the same roof with a superior chief when sick, and he must—to use a slang expression—get out. You will gather from what I have just said that the sickness of a chief forthwith made his house *tapu* against all intruders, save of the same or superior rank. To break such a *tapu*, even unwittingly, was to bring down on the offender's head *te makutu* bewitchment, of which, ten to one, he would die.

As I soon saw what a hold Ngatai's spirit-warning had taken of Te Pirete, and as there was no reason why he should not remove himself from the dangerous *tapu* roof-tree under which he now slept, I told him he might take himself off whenever he liked, and that I would come and visit him in his new hut. So he forthwith did take himself from under the dangerous *tapu*, and did not break it even for one other night—in fact, I had no sooner turned my back upon the tent than he was outside it!

Oh, spirit of Ngatai! why ate you not your *kumara* in your native paradise in contented happiness with those around you? Was the coveted pipe of tobacco *not* a pipe of peace, and why did ye wander back among the living of your tribe?

'He came to me again last night', said Te Pirete to me a few mornings afterwards when I was paying him my daily visit *en route* to the forest; 'he came to me last night, and said I must come and wait upon him in the land of spirits, and so you see I *must* go—quickly go.'

Imagine how wide I opened my eyes on hearing this announcement made so calmly—in fact, I was very nearly bursting into a fit of laughter; but fortunately, looking more intently at his face, I saw a stricken gravity written thereon which convinced me it was anything but a laughing matter.

The change which had already taken place was startling, and I beheld it with wonder. His bodily health appeared to be all right, and his burns were healing rapidly, but I there and then became convinced I had a new and unknown enemy to grapple with—one which brought home to me the words, 'Who can minister to a mind diseased?'

On feeling his pulse, lo! it was evident that already Ngatai's spirit had begun to do its work, for the current of poor Te Pirete's blood flowed in too fast a stream, and pulsated in too quick a beat.

'Oh, nonsense!' I said to myself, 'the man has had an exciting dream—passed a restless night—it is only a nervous fit—and after a good sleep he will be all right again.'

I went away firmly believing so, and thought no more about it whilst digging away at our canoe.

But Pama did not look upon it in this way when I told my story at our evening meal. He shook his head and gravely said he did not much like the looks of it, but to-morrow would settle it one way or the other.

'To-morrow settle it one way or the other! What in the name of wonder do you mean? Do you mean to say that to-morrow Te Pirete is either to be all right, or, as you would say, a gone 'coon?'

'Well, sir, he may not be dead, but', added Pama, as if talking of a most ordinary circumstance, 'he may be just as good as dead, for these Maoris, sir, can die off in a couples of shakes just whenever they have taken it into their heads that they *ought* to die off.'

I could not help thinking that Pama had got a good touch himself of poor Te Pirete's complaint, and that he too was bewitched.

But as I recalled that strange, mysterious look which had fallen upon Te Pirete's face a lurking uneasiness arose

within me, and so I slipped away when our meal was
finished to Pirete's hut, wondering whether a good sleep
and a good meal, and probably a nice smoke, would have
made my patient all right again, or whether Pama's fore-
bodings were to be realized.

Alas! I found Te Pirete's bronze cheeks warmed with
a feverish glow which could not be overlooked.

'Oh! young Æsculapius, to whom shall the victory be
given? To thy art, to save, or to the spirit of Ngatai to
destroy?'

It was thus I mentally questioned myself as I passed
slowly home with grave misgivings.

And as I so passed from the chief's hut to Pama's *whare*
I did conclude that there were a great many more things
than I had ever dreamt of in my verdant philosophy!

'There is no mistake about it', said I to Pama on getting
home, 'Te Pirete has got a touch of fever.'

'Oh, he has, has he? then I'll tell you what we may as
well do, sir. You were helping me to get out stuff enough
to make Ngatai's coffin, and it will just save a good bit
of trouble to get out the stuff for *two,* for I can tell you,
as sure as you are standing there, a *pair* of *coffins* will be
wanted, for Te Pirete *is* a gone 'coon.'

And Pama sat himself down to smoke his pipe, and
as he puffed away he continued speaking to us through
the open doorway in the partition which divided our end
of the *whare* from his:

'That is always the way, sirs, with these strange people
—they can die off whenever they take it into their heads.
When I was in the North, before coming down here, I
killed off a young woman in the most innocent way
possible before I knew what I was about, all through this
tapu of theirs. I was travelling from Te Horeke to Okaihau,
and was taking a rest at an old *pa,* when I saw this girl,
one of our party, eating a *kumara,* for you know they eat
rather nice raw on a warm day, and it was such a fine-
looking one, I said, "Where did you get that fine *kumara?*"
When she told me I stupidly said, "Don't you know that

is a *wahi tapu* (sacred ground), and the great Te Rewi
was buried there?" Lord! sirs, the *kumara* dropped from
her hand as if she had been shot. She would have screamed,
but she was just dead terrified beyond screaming. She
had no voice to scream with, and, what is more, she never
got it again, sirs. She just went and lay down in an old
whare, and *she* was a gone 'coon in eight-and-forty hours.
Now mark my word, sirs, you'll see that Te Pirete will die
himself off just the same way as sure as I am sitting here—
you'll see if he don't, that's all. It's not fright that will kill
him off, but just that Ngatai's *atua* (spirit) has come to
him, and he has got it into his head he must go to Ngatai,
and, by the Lord Harry! see if he don't.'

And the next morning, as we came home from our
work and visited Te Pirete, and saw the marvellously
sudden change that had come over him, we agreed with
Pama in thinking that the summons of Ngatai was one
which was going to be obeyed, and that Te Pirete had
fully made up his mind to 'die himself from off the face
of the earth', as Pama had put it.

But we certainly were not prepared for the suddenness
with which this was accomplished.

Only one more day had passed when Te Pirete's face
became still more marvellously changed, though it was
but three days since he had received the midnight
summons.

And when midnight came again the death-wail broke
upon the stillness of the night, rending the air. And the
wail was caught up, and we heard it in faint and fainter
sounds as it was repeated away up the length and breadth
of the Waiomu valley.

'Did you hear that?' shouted out Pama from his bed;
'that's Te Pirete that's dead. He's been and done it—knew
he would quite well—they always will, sirs, when they
once fairly take it into their heads—such a queer people,
sirs.'

Rangi, who, on the first death-wail awakening her,
had jumped out of bed and rushed off in the direction of
Te Pirete's *whare,* soon made her reappearance.

It was little use for her to go to Te Pirete's *whare*—his death had already been telegraphed by the voice from one end of the valley to the other.

Alas! poor old Kanini! More *tapu* is your doom—more of the lugubrious nose-rubbing to be done over again with all comers, crouching by Te Pirete lying in state—steeped in *tapu*, feeding with hands behind your back from a provision platform.

Yes, his brother-chiefs enjoined upon him a long and strict tapu to propitiate the evil gods and avert their wrath from the chiefs of the Ngati Tamatera.

And now we saw all the funereal ceremonies done over again. Those who had *tangi*-d over Ngatai had to come and *tangi* over Te Pirete. The throats of even the old women waxed hoarse; they had barely an unscarified square inch of skin left upon which to operate with the sharp-edged shell—at least, if they had, it was not visible, and must have been searched for under the short waist-to-knee mat which adorned their persons. One thing was certain, if the mourners wailed and scarified well, so did they eat. They displayed wonderful energy in the feasting line—went at it tooth-and-nail, and never gave in. But the provisions of the tribe nearly did; they were as nearly as possible eaten out of house and home, they had hardly a kit of even seed-potatoes left; as for *kumara*, that was a vegetable of the past, and of the future after the next season's crop came in, for they would have never another kit of them until the next crop was ripe.

As I have already stated, poor old Kanini was steeped in *tapu* all over, and consigned to a hermit's life; he was so awfully *tapu* that hardly any one dared go near him. I, too, had become *tapu* on account of having handled the two sick chiefs, so *I* could go and see the old man, sit beside him, and even go into his *whare* and under the sacred roof-tree. We were both in the same boat, and so could pull together. And many were the long evenings I spent with the poor be-*tapu*'d hermit. Pama, too, was *tapu* all over—hideously *tapu*—for had he not helped the old chief

in putting both Ngatai and Te Pirete into those two coffins
we had made? for we had scraped together 'stuff' enough
to make the pair of them which he had predicted would
be wanted. My *tapu* proved a most happy thing, and came
in most opportunely during the deluge of Maoris which
flooded Waiomu, for had it not been for my *tapu* we
should not have been able to keep our *whare* our own.
Happily it also became *tapu* because I was *tapu,* and only
Kanini dared enter it.

An amusing incident occurred one day which gave us
a grand haul for dinner. Some pots of food— most
capacious pots—were boiling away in front of our door.
We had just returned after our day's work in the forest
and I was sharply peckish, and ready to do full justice
to Rangi's supper. I knew the *kumara* were fast running
out, and a most tempting one was just beginning to show
high and dry in the pot I saw boiling, and I could not
resist appropriating it. As I stretched out my hand to
take it a chorus of yells from all the women superintending
the cooking met my ear—such awfully diabolical yells
that I nearly let my prize drop out of my hand.

Alas! too late the warning; before I understood its
meaning I had touched the food, and had unwittingly
appropriated not only that tempting *kumara,* but the
whole contents of the huge pot—yes, the whole blessed
contents—for the sole use of the inmates of Pama House!

What native dare eat of food which had been touched
by a *tapu* hand? That night a supper fell to our share a
dozen times larger than we could eat.

Nor could I console the bereaved ones who had lost
their supper (and who had to wait with what patience they
could until a fresh supply was ready) by giving them a
peace-offering in the shape of a pipe of tobacco to smoke,
for everything in the *whare* was *tapu.* To smoke a pipe
filled with tobacco out of that *tapu whare* would almost
have been as bad as eating a *kumara* grown in a *wahi tapu.*

The great concourse of natives which the double death
in the tribe had brought to mourn and feast at Waiomu

gave us the opportunity of becoming acquainted with the Maori aristocracy of the neighbourhood, but, what was of much more interest and importance, enabled us to acquire a complete insight into the manners and customs of the race.

At the end of three weeks, during which time this wake of wakes lasted, and which proved to us the Maori capacity for stowing away pork and potatoes, and especially *kumara*, Te Rite had so far recovered that he was able to go to his own village, a couple of miles down the gulf.

Hereafter I shall narrate the return that was made to me for doctoring him. Ere we quitted Waiomu his tribe rendered the two Rangatira Pakehas an essential service.

F

CHAPTER VIII

Maori Philosophy

AT last our village settled down to its wonted quietness,
minus the chiefs, who were now in their Elysium
eating *kumara* and smoking pipes for evermore; minus
also their whole stock of winter provisions, which the
funeral feasting had fairly exhausted, rendering it necessary to have recourse to the *dernier ressort*—fern-root,
flavoured with fish and *pipi*. But to two individuals of
the Maori community—the widow chieftainess of the
two dead men—a blank had been made which to them
could never be filled.

Hard indeed was their case—in the full bloom of young
womanhood to be laid on the non-matrimonial shelf for
evermore. But such was their fate; had there been any
younger brothers of the dead chiefs the widows would
have descended to them, whether previously provided with
wives or not—polygamy, it must be remembered, being
the order of the day. But in the two cases in question there
were no surviving brothers upon whom the husband's
mantle could fall, so they were doomed to waste their
widow fragrance on the desert Maori air—to use a figure
of speech—and the poor things had not even the satisfaction of succeeding to the personal effects of their defunct
lords, for even as they themselves had become matri-
monially *tapu*, so had everything belonging to the dead
chiefs become irrevocably *tapu*.

It mattered not how valuable the property left behind —their guns and blankets and highly-prized and beautiful *kaitaka* mats—everything at their death met the same *tapu*-absorbing fate. On the fence around their graves could be seen hanging all their late treasures—wives excepted, of course.

If at any time in their newly-attained paradise they fancied any of these their late possessions, they had only to come, in spirit, and take them away, there on the fence they would find everything sacredly preserved—I ought rather to say sacrificed to their manes.

And all these coveted treasures hang as safely there as if lodged in strongest tower and watched with strictest guard. What Maori would dare the *tapu*, even if he could possess himself of all? We have but to think of the poor girl who ate of a *wahi tapu kumara*, and who would be so mad as ever to dream of despoiling a dead chief's tomb?

No; the coveted double-barrelled gun may rust to pieces, the *kaitaka* mat drop rotting piecemeal to the ground, but no sacrilegious hand will dare touch either the one or the other—a shield of impenetrable *tapu* covers all.

History repeats itself—so we hear—every day; the customs of one race are found repeated in another, however far apart and apparently unconnected.

In after years (having done one decade of pioneer settling, and starting to see the world before doing a second) I found the Maori was only doing as the Turk did.

When I stood on the shores of the Bosphorus, now thirty years ago, did I not see there tombs decked with the effects of the defunct, only, there, *tapu* was of no avail to hold sacred the cashmere shawl and diamond-trimmed *turboush*. Strongest door and strictest guard had to be set there, or these tombs would not have remained long unrifled—it was not likely when grand tiaras of diamonds tempted men to sacrilege.

And if you cross over to Scutari I can tell you something more savouring of the ways of Maoridom. As you

ascend to gaze on the wonderful panorama from Mount
Burgurla, perchance it may happen to you some day that
your dragoman may point out to you, as he did to me, a
spot, saying, 'There stood a small summer palace of Sultan'
—Heaven knows what his name—I forget now—'in it he
died, and it was burned down with all it contained', so
that no one should ever make use of what, in fact, had
become *tapu* by his death!

'Tis true that was done on the Asiatic shore of the
Bosphorus—'tis but a step to the European shore! Yes,
history is evidently given to much repetition. So perhaps
'tis but a step from ancient Orientalism to primitive customs in Polynesia!

Winter, as it slipped past, fulfilled the promise of its
early commencement, the weather being truly delightful.

How people get spoiled, to be sure! I actually now-a-
days hear complaining grumblers growling at our winter.
Don't I wish them back again to 'Northern climes
abhorred' to renew their remembrance by actually feeling
the abhorrence? They have so long lived under our
glorious sunshine that they remember not the gloomy
days which hung over them in their youth—vile fogs, end-
less rain, the sun making frantic efforts to pierce the
murkiness, and beating an ignominious retreat. Oh! how
it weighed upon me when I revisited my 'ain kintrie' after
a decade of blissful sunshine! That long-ago first winter,
and our work in the forest, was a new revelation of delight
to me. We built grand *châteaux en Espagne* when digging
out our canoe and converted it into a very argosy, and
sailed away in it—well, paddled if you like it better—full
of our young and hopeful aspirations. Few were the days
we could not go to our work. We were up at daylight.
Rangi's pot of pork and potatoes and pannikin of tea were
always ready, and the little kit full of cold *kumara* for our
luncheon. She was wise in her generation, and when she
saw the *kumara* being swept away by that hurricane of
funereal feasting, she had smuggled into our *tapu whare*
a grand supply, and, of course, no one then dare eat them

except ourselves. Our cold *kumara*, a drink of the clear spring-water that trickled past our log, and we were very kings—we envied no man. Hard work is such a grand appetizer when it goes with a good constitution, and with fine keen bracing air, and last, not least, a mind full of hope—these are the sauces that make simple fare rich.

We had our small luxuries too. Every now and again a pig had to be killed and corned down, and then we had a couple of fresh-meat days. Rangi ventured on soups made in a fearful and wonderful way, but we thought them—stunning, only I don't think that word was invented then. As a treat of a most extraordinary kind on rare occasions, she gave us one ship's biscuit to be divided amongst us, and as she placed it on our simple board she would beam all over in a wonderful glow of smiles, as who would say—'There! haven't I given you something nice to-night?' And she was right; we did think it so, and ate it accordingly.

And we had our small trials too in the curtailment of our great luxuries, for the principal of these came to an end during our sojourn at Waiomu. One morning a very medicinal odour arose from our pannikins as Rangi placed them before us with the remark in a very commiserating tone—

'*Kua pau te ti.*'

Too true! the tea had run out! But the Pama substitute of wild mint was served instead, and—gratefully accepted. The difference, however, was that Rangi's two Pakehas no longer looked forward to their pannikin of tea as the one nice little treat in store.

It is so easy to become epicurean!

If we had only been living in a civilized land with Maori customs we should have had a chance of laying in a fresh supply of tea on easy terms, as you will gather from what I am now about to tell you. One morning as we were starting to the forest we observed an unusual bustle in the settlement, and evident preparations going on for some expedition. We noted, however, that although almost every native was gun in hand, there was not the usual accompaniment of the cartouche-box, so the inference to be drawn was that the tribe was not going out on the warpath. The fact was, they were all about to start on a *taua* [*muru*] or raid—a robbing visit to a neighbouring friendly tribe connected with them by marriage, as Pama informed us.

'But in the name of wonder,' I asked, 'what does it mean? An expedition to rob their own relations and friends? Why, what *does* a *taua* [*muru*] mean?'

'It is great fun', responded Pama, 'except to those upon whom the *taua* is going to be inflicted. You ought to go, sir—you might make a haul of a fine *kaitaka* mat. They have just got news that Te Tara's daughter, who is married to one of the Ngati Porou chiefs, has been misbehaving herself. The young lady has been found out in a love intrigue with another young chief. Now you must know that if her husband had been a very much bigger chief, and his tribe more powerful than ours, perhaps he might just have put a tomahawk into the young lady's head, and a bullet into the gentleman's. But in this case he dare not use his tomahawk, though it is just possible he may have used a stick, but the gossip does not say the young lady has had a welting.'

'And is the tribe off on a *taua,* as you call it, on the strength of the possible fact that the husband has thrashed the girl, and is he to be robbed because he has punished the guilty?'

'No, sir, that's not the way of it at all. The thrashing has nothing to do with it, but it is the custom of these queer people that the girl's relations and friends go and rob the husband.'

'The devil it is! then all I can say is that inscrutable are the ways and customs of the Maori. Explain for goodness' sake. Why, here is a man who has the misfortune—the dreadful domestic calamity—of an unfaithful wife, and he is *taua*'d into the bargain by way of condolence from her relations. Unriddle me this riddle, O sphinx Pama!'

'What the Maoris say is this, sir, that if the husband had been kind and good to his wife, and treated her properly, she would not have gone astray; therefore it is his fault that she has misbehaved, and they punish him by a *taua,* and not only him, but his tribe too.'

'But you don't mean to say that the tribe submit to be robbed without having a fight for it?'

'Yes I do, sir. You just go and see. If they know beforehand they may hide a lot of things, but if they don't, and the *taua* is down upon them before they know where they are, you will see them just sitting quietly squatted on the ground on their mats, if they have been able to get hold of them first, and they will sit and never budge an inch whilst the other fellows are helping themselves and walking away with everything they can lay their hands upon.'

And so I lifted up my voice and said, 'Oh, Horatio! there *are*——'

Bother the quotation! And why should *not* the Maori have a strange philosophy?

'*E tika nei!*' That is true indeed.

CHAPTER IX

Farewell to Waiomu

THE longest *tapu* must have an end, and poor old Kanini has at last dispensed with his provision platform, and now luxuriates in the use of his own fingers, and is allowed to feed himself. Faithfully had the old man kept all *tapu* observances, though in reality he did not believe in them one jot or tittle. I have already stated he was a man of great intellectual power, far in advance of all his own surroundings and of his own day, and certainly had buried long ago in the tomb of unbelief *tapu* itself. In proof I shall narrate an incident.

My friend was a great phrenologist and a practical one, and had wished, above all things, to be allowed to manipulate Kanini's head and take its measurements. Now the most *tapu* of all things is a chief's head, and when the proposition was first made to him, he, of course, gave a decided *'Kahore'* ('No'). But as we became more intimately acquainted with him, and ultimately knew that he looked upon *tapu* as so much humbug, my friend kept renewing his application until at last the old man, in a soft moment, said, *'Ae pea'*, which literally means 'Yes—perhaps', but in reality always means 'Yes'—at all events amongst the young ladies when they give that reply to a suitor. So it came about that, according to arrangements made with Kanini, his wives being absent on a *kumara*-seeking expedition, we invaded the old man's *whare* after midnight, and he submitted his sacred head to be pawed—phrenologically speaking—all over. I would not have given much for Kanini's status in his tribe if any member of it could have seen what took place that night, but no more convincing proof could be given as to the old chief being generations in advance of the day in which he was living.

His evenings were invariably spent with us, the old man holding most animated conversations with Pama, and discussing, in the most intelligent manner, all the habits and customs of his race, from the abominable bore of the *tapu*—which he next thing to anathematised—downwards. Dire was the amount of questioning to which he was subjected by his Rangatira Pakehas, but his good nature never gave in. It was, indeed, a pleasure to hold converse with him, or to look at his calm, noble countenance and head, and his bright clear eye, with intelligence beaming from it. His calm low voice fell quietly and pleasantly on the ear, and we were lost in wonder when we looked upon the old man sitting so sedately by our side, and listened to his placid voice, remembering that this pattern of present propriety had many a time and oft jumped savagely high, with distorted countenance, leading a war-dance. Or yelled forth unearthly yells in concert with his tribe, worked up to frenzied heat by a war harangue delivered by him. Ah, old man, it had been better had innocent talking only been the end of it, and not eating!

No, we won't believe it, Pama—get out with you; we are not going to believe these cannibal-feast yarns of yours.

No; the Kanini to us is the civilized savage we have ever found him—the one bright particular star of his race. No black cloud shall hang over the halo with which we have surrounded his white head; we ignore the past, and, once and for all, Kanini is to us the Kanini of Waiomu in the year of grace one thousand eight hundred and forty!

And pray who shall say, after all, that it is not much better to eat than to be eaten?

Therefore Kanini was preserved to us to minister to our winter evenings' amusement and instruction in that year of grace on the shores of Te Hauraki.

And here I would fain say a word in kind remembrance of the 'savage faculty'—the phrase is not mine, but Harriet Martineau's, who coined it in her Egyptian travels—the savage faculty as I knew it, and as others of the very earliest days, like myself, now all so rapidly passing away, also knew it, of the Maori race as known to the pioneer settlers of the land, and not as known to those of later days, who arrive in the colony and have on their tongues the talk of the '*nigger* element', and who have no knowledge and no ideas of Maori character, save as gathered from these later days, when a new generation has sprung into being, whose acts and deeds on the warpath when the opposing races met face to face have been the gauge by which Maori character has been judged. To these newcomers the aborigines are an abomination, a delusion, and a snare.

They know not, have never heard of, and to few, indeed, is known, the high chivalrous honour which characterized the Maori in the early wars we had with them. Hereafter I shall narrate such strange incidents of their high chivalry that many who read will simply disbelieve, but what I set down will nonetheless be true. I shall be writing of the Maori of forty years ago. I claim to say that a description of the Maori character of that day is worth preserving for the history of the race, so that the Maori of the future may know that his ancestors possessed high and noble qualities, which, alas! Pakeha civilization has relegated to the past. Much as has been written about the Maori, I have never yet seen revealed in print to the public certain high traits of character unique in the history of the races of the world.

'*Kua pau te huka*', said mild-voiced Rangi one morning as she placed before us our pannikins of mint-tea, which informed us that time, which had kept slipping away, had used up all the sugar! Mint-tea *in puris natura-libus* would not go down, so 'we twa' had to pay the penalty for being so fastidious by just falling back upon good pure spring-water. Pork and potatoes and good spring-water for breakfast, and good spring-water and potatoes and pork when we came home at night, were the changes we rang, and we had to make the best of it. But hunger is such a leveller of daintily-reared appetites, and hard labour in the open air so rears up hunger, that we did as much justice to Rangi's simple fare as if it had been Orakei Bay *ragoût* of happy memory!

And our own canoe, in which we *were* to paddle, how did it get on? The canoe was now well formed outside, and pretty well hollowed out inside, so much so that now it was not deemed safe to reduce the dimensions of the log any more until it was dragged out of the forest. The log had to be sent over some rather steep places, and it must be able to stand a good blow with impunity should it strike against any rock or tree before reaching the water's edge.

Many had been the visits paid by the Maoris to the forest where we were at work, for our log was really not modelled as a canoe but like a boat, with regular bow and stern. Amongst our visitors latterly had been Te Rite, lately my patient, and also his father, Taraia, an old warrior of dread renown. They had watched with great attention the progress of our work, and learning from Pama the log must now be dragged out before any further work could be done upon it, Taraia and his son waited upon the two Rangatira Pakehas one night to tender the services of the tribe to drag out the *waka Pakeha* (white man's canoe) in gratitude—no, I must not use that word, for it exists not in the Maori vocabulary —it was *'te utu mo te rongoa a te rata'*—the payment for the medicine of the doctor!

As may be well believed, no more appropriate or well-timed fee could have been tendered, and as 'nothing for

nothing' is Maori philosophy, we did not attempt to alter
the logic, nor was the fee refused.

It thus came about that the explosion of the half-keg
of gunpowder dragged out our canoe, for after four days'
work it lay on the beach in front of our door all safe and
sound.

And on the same day there were also piled in front of
our door some forty kits—nearly a ton—of the delicious
taro, and, tied with a flax-leaf by the hind leg to a stake
stuck into the ground, was a huge porker grunting.

Of this provision-offering Pama was supposed to be
an equal recipient, as he had in many small ways performed services to the old chief and his son. Of course,
we had to make a considerable distribution of pipes and
tobacco; indeed, it was a kind of understood thing that
the value of the food-offering was paid back again to go
amongst the members of the tribe as just a little palm-
salve for dragging out the canoe.

And so now we had no longer to take our walk into
the beautiful forest through evergreen foliage of brightest tints, fern-trees, and *nikau* palms waving overhead,
and flowing creepers—ah, the beauty of our forests!—no
longer had we now the grand commanding view across
the Hauraki to where Ponui stands sentinel at the
entrance of the land-locked waters that lead to Waitemata's shore. How often, when resting from our work,
we had gazed across that landscape, all that then showed
life in the gulf was but the speck of the *raupo* sail of a
waka Maori on few and rare occasions; daily now,
steamers plough up those waters.

Our work was now only a stone's throw from our
own door on the beach in front, and in a few days we
had given the few finishing touches which removed the
superfluous wood which we had left to enable it to stand
the rough usage it was bound to get on being dragged
out of the forest.

I well remember how one morning before breakfast,
when I was cutting with an adze at the outside, and my

fellow-worker was fining down the floor inside, I
remarked to him I thought he was shaving away rather
too much, that if it was left somewhat rough and thick
it would be all the better, as being easier to stand upon if
rough under foot, and if thick less likely to be harmed
by hard bumps on a rock. He prided himself on his large
organ of cautiousness, and would not admit but that
there was plenty of thickness yet to come and go upon,
and he went on cutting away. Alas! the words were
hardly out of his mouth when, lo! the tool went right
through the bottom of the canoe! With what a ridiculous
face of consternation he looked up at me! It was so utterly
comical and I laughed so heartily that at last he could
not refrain from keeping me company. I rather enjoyed
the small catastrophe, as it gave me such a crow over
him, for he had always been at me with his 'Take care
what you are about; I am afraid of that small organ of
cautiousness of yours.'

But the account was now settled for evermore; in
after years when he used that phrase to me I had the
whip hand, and it was, 'Do you happen to remember
that fine morning when you first saw daylight through
the bottom of the Waiomu?' for of course we christened
our canoe by that name. The hole in the bottom, after
all, was of no consequence; the skilful hand of Pama
soon cut out the thin part, and meeting plenty of thickness of wood close alongside, he fitted in a piece which
lasted as long as the canoe, and it never leaked a panni-
kinful.

It was fortunate indeed that we had taken Pama's
advice and had gone to our forest work, for no other
sawyers ever came near to cut up more planking for King
Wepiha—in fact, he had to send some from Herekino to
enable Pama to finish the boat he had in hand, so but
for our own canoe we should not have been able to go
and take possession of our island home at Waitemata.

Winter was waning when at last both Pama's boat
and our canoe were finished. Pama had to deliver the

boat to King Wepiha at Herekino, so we determined to avail ourselves of the opportunity to transport our effects there in it, as the canoe would not be large enough.

So the time had now come when we must bid farewell to Waiomu; our sojourn on the shore of Te Hauraki had run out; we must turn our backs upon the Maori village where we had spent so pleasant and happy, and— I think I may safely style it—romantic a life.

We must bid farewell to the Ngati Tamatera and their grand old chief.

And that farewell was not made without feelings of the most sincere regret on our part, for our sojourn in the primitive Maori village had not been in vain.

Irrespective of having become owners of a canoe of our own fabrication, we had acquired a most valuable insight into native character which was yet to stand us in good stead in later years, though we little thought so at that time.

We had witnessed scenes which would live for evermore in our memories—for evermore even when old age would stamp our now young heads with blanched hair, even like the old chief's we loved so well.

A never-to-be-blotted-out epoch of our lives when we were pioneers amongst a people whose manners and customs were doomed in our own day to change and fade away before the civilizing agency of a Saxon colony then taking root, and which was destined to overshadow the land to the Maori for evermore, bringing, as it ever brings, a never-ending night to an aboriginal race of darker blood.

The poor old Kanini had evidently become strongly attached to his two Pakehas; this fact had been patent to us for a long time. He had ever been a solitary man amongst his own people, but he could not be with us too much; he gravitated to us every evening with an irresistible impulse; he had found meet companions in two young Pakehas—he, an old Maori!

Is it to be wondered at, that, estimating his high

native worth, and the bright intelligence we had found under that tattooed face, we were moved to severe regret at parting with him?

But to us the world was all in the future, to the old chief it was all in the past.

'Tis ever so; the world's a stage, and the actors thereon play their little part, and having played it do make their exit.

The tattooed Kanini was leaving the stage of life, his two Rangatira Pakehas were advancing on to it.

And so they needs must part.

Pama's new boat and the *waka Pakeha* are afloat on the waters of Te Hauraki, abreast the village of Waiomu.

We have shaken hands with nearly the whole Ngati Tamatera tribe.

The old Kanini sat muffled in his *kaitaka* mat on the beach.

'*E noho nei?*' we said to him in a sad voice. 'You will stay there, won't you?' as we shook hands with him.

'*Haere—haere*' ('Go—go'), came from him in a low voice.

Such are the Maori words in which farewells are made. The whole tribe followed us down to the boat tendering kind offices; we put off with a well-wishing '*Haere*' from all.

But he sat on the shore, that old chief, all alone; who shall say how much more lonely that untutored mind was then than throughout his whole life?

For was he not parting with those whose society had revealed to him how much more he was fitted by nature to take his place and move among civilized men than among his own people? Did he not then sigh as he had often done when seated with his two Pakehas on winter nights, when the burthen of his sighs had been, 'Ah that I were a Pakeha!' and when a sad sorrowfulness would fall upon him.

How much more sad now as he sits on that shore, and we say our parting words—

'*E noho nei?*' You will stay there, won't you?

Yes, grey-haired old chief, you must still remain there.

For the cold snow of age has left your head with too whitened locks for you to commence a new journey in life.

Vain aspirations—vain regrets!

E noho! e noho! chief of the Ngati Tamatera, and nature's nobleman.

E noho! yet a little while, and the gates of thy simple paradise will be opened to you. *E noho!*

He sat alone with his sorrow on the shore of the Hauraki, gazing vacantly at the ebbing waters as they flowed at his feet.

He sat there an old battered chief, the emblem of a living race and a past history, which is doomed to disappear and be forgotten.

Haere—haere—Go—go, Pakehas, and pitch your tent on the solitary place of Motu-Korea, for you have found a new home—you are the pioneers of a race coming from afar to make a new nation, and raise a new history.

E noho—Oh, Chief!

Haere—Oh, Pakehas!

BOOK FOURTH

How a New Colony is Born to an Old Nation

CHAPTER I

The Two Pioneer Pakehas of the Waitemata

IT was on the evening of a lovely day in early spring that a small boat with two sprit-sails set, one on each side, could be seen towing a canoe over an expanse of water which more resembled a lake than what it really was—an inlet of the sea.

The breeze was fair but light, barely keeping the sails full—a tantalizing breeze, which always promised to freshen up, yet never did—a breeze which you would fain believe made the boat go faster than it would if you took to the oars, and yet you did not feel quite at rest on that point. However, there was nothing to be done but either to furl the sails and unstep the masts and take to the oars, or to be content to keep creeping lazily along and make the best of the breeze, such as it was.

Two of the occupants of the boat were evidently much more interested in the scenery around them than in the rate at which the boat was sailing. Little wonder if they were so engrossed, for the landscape was one of surpassing beauty. The boat had just rounded a promontory, in doing which the travellers had opened up an entirely new view.

A sheet of water lay stretched before them about fourteen miles long by about six broad. From the travellers' point of view it was landlocked. Here and there openings could be seen, but more distant land filled up the background. These passages appeared to wander round little islands, creating a desire to be able to explore them all.

At the western extremity of the inlet one of these little islands lay in mid-channel. The most picturesque of little rounded mountains reared itself, as if guarding the passage, and, proud of its own beauty, was not in the least ashamed that it lay right in the fairway, and blocked up the centre of the passage and the view beyond. It was quite evident, as the boat headed for the centre of the island, and not towards one of the passages on either side, that to the island the travellers were bound.

The right-hand shore of the inlet rose steeply from the water's edge, save here and there where little bays broke into the continuity of the coast-line. In these indentations —hardly to be termed bays—there always could be seen a little plateau of level land stretching from the shore to the base of the hills, which then rose abruptly.

The eye rested with delight on the evergreen foliage of primeval forest, wonderfully rich in the varied contrast of its colours. Although the season was but early spring, winter had laid its hand so gently on all nature that it changed but little the aspect of the woods, which ever smiled, arrayed in a garment of richest verdure.

And to Nature alone was due all the beauty of the scenery our travellers were revelling in, for as yet her reign here had been undisturbed and all but supreme.

As the boat skirted alongshore the eye was able to detect every few miles that one of these diminutive valleys nestling at the base of the hills was less rich and beautiful in the colour of its vegetation. It owed its change of appearance to the clearing hand of man, for there he dwelt in an uncivilized and primitive state. Canoes on the beach and low huts on the shore told our travellers that they were passing native villages, and they seemed to scrutinize more keenly those spots showing signs of life, as if they wished to impress the respective localities well on the memory.

The boat meanwhile had its head steadily steered for the still-distant island, and gradually drew towards mid-channel, and the opposite shore became more distinct.

It was not nearly so beautiful as that on the right hand:

it was destitute of forest, and was of an open, undulating character, resembling uplands. In the direction of the island it opened into a deep bay, and at its head, the land being low, the eye failed to detect where the waters ended and land commenced. Fatigued with the search, the eye ran along the gradually-rising high land, which ended in a bold headland just opposite the little island. This promontory showed a face of yellow sandstone, and at its extremity it was crowned by a magnificent clump of trees, while smaller shrubs hung over the edge of the cliff, the green foliage thrown into startling relief by the yellow background.

As you gazed on this plumed headland of exquisite beauty you now and again laboured under the optical illusion that it was moving; you thought at one time it was nearer the island, and then again farther off. You imagined it was making obeisances to the little island, and endeavouring, with the most graceful and quiet movements, to attract attention towards its pretty plumed head and command admiration. It was in vain the eye wandered away from this plumed headland to the bare promontory behind to make certain of the perfect stability of the whole. You found yourself again looking at and believing in the nodding headland, and half feared, if you took your eye away, the next time you looked the headland—plume and all—would be found to have thrown itself into the arms of the little island's mountain, and hidden all its beauties in the shadow of that mountain's bosom.

The boat had now gained mid-channel, and had lessened the distance to the island by one-half since we saw it rounding the opening, now seven miles away. The travellers thought they had come at least two-thirds of the way, and that they were almost at the end of their voyage. The island looked close ahead of them, not more than a couple of miles off, for they had not yet become accustomed to calculate distance correctly in that clear Southern hemisphere, and their impatience was bridging over too quickly the yet intervening space.

And now, to add to the deception, the sun sank behind the little island's little mountain, throwing its shadow over the water and illumining the outline of the whole island so vividly that it seemed close at hand, and that a few oar-strokes would bring them to its shore.

There is still time, however, before the shore is reached to pay a visit on board the boat and see in what manner it is freighted.

There were seven persons on board—three Pakehas, and four of the crew, who were Maoris; the Pakehas occupied the stern-sheets, one of them steering. Of the Maoris two were in attendance watching the sails; but as this did not entail much attention, one of them was dreamily smoking a pipe, whilst the other was cutting up some tobacco ready for his turn at the said pipe, for they had only one between them. The other two of the crew were wrapped in sleep in the bottom of the boat, one of them having pillowed his head on a grindstone, the other having selected more wisely and chosen a bag of salt. In the bottom of the boat could be seen in strange confusion the poles of a tent and the tent itself rolled into a bundle —why this was not preferred to the grindstone Maori ideas alone can say. Then there was a sack of flour, which would have made a nice comfortable pillow; then the bag of salt, some large and small three-legged gipsy pots, a frying-pan, a spade and a grubbing-hoe, a hatchet, some kits of potatoes, *kumara* and maize, and one of corned pork, as the head and jowl sufficiently demonstrated; a large and very capacious wooden chest, half a keg of negrohead tobacco, and a bundle, through the corners of which could be seen striped cotton shirts, blankets, &c., and there has now been summed up pretty nearly what constituted the ballast of the boat on that voyage.

And truly it was but a very primitive and scanty turn-out with which to make a first settlement, as was evidently the intention of the occupants of the boat, because with no other could any one be wandering so far beyond the limits of civilization with so large a stock of commodities.

No huts on the shore or canoes on the beach had been seen by the travellers for some time. These seemed to have been all left behind; and the boat, slipping quietly through the water before the gentle but fair wind whilst nearing its haven, increased the solitude of the surrounding scene.

Hark to that sharp, quick bark! A noble dog, half bloodhound, half mastiff, which must have lain concealed till now, bounded from the bow of the boat, and, smelling land, thus proclaimed the boat's near approach to it, and rushed to the stern sheets to tell the news to his masters, and then away again to place his paws on the boat's gunwale at the bow and bark again.

The boat was now under the shadow of the little island's little mountain. The sun had nearly set; the breeze no longer filled the sails; they began to flap against the masts. The steersman summoned the crew to their oars, the two sleepers were aroused, the luxurious grindstone and bag of salt pillows can no longer be indulged in, the pipe of lazy peace must be put aside, and the four natives twisted their mats round their waists, and having first furled the sails and unstepped the masts, took their seats, and their naked bronze shoulders soon strained to the oars.

The canoe towing astern made it a heavy pull, but they gave way with a will. We had only to look at the hound in the bow of the boat to know that the island was all but reached; he no longer went jumping along to expend his impatience in barking visits to his masters; he only changed his paws from one side of the bow of the boat to the other; his whining had changed into shorter and quicker barking; and at last, unable to restrain himself, he jumped on the gunwale, prepared himself for a spring, and plunged into the water, and by the time he had reached the shore the keel of the boat grazed on the beach—the island was gained.

The Maoris adroitly slipped out of their mats, and *puris naturalibus* they were over the boat's side in a moment and dragged it up as far as they could, just sufficient to keep it on even keel. Three of them commenced at once to carry the things on shore, the fourth started off in search of fresh water and drift-wood, and before his companions had finished their work of emptying the boat he had returned and had a brisk fire burning and a pot of water nearly boiling.

The Pakehas meanwhile had chosen a spot on which to pitch their tent; they had not been over-fastidious in their selection, as the shades of evening were rapidly closing, for there twilight has but little more than a name, and but a short interval elapses after the sun sets ere night prevails.

The stars were already shining brightly, telling the travellers to make the best of their time.

The tent was soon pitched, and whatever was wanted for the night, and anything that would have been damaged had a shower fallen, carried into it from the boat. It was only the elements that had to be feared, and the beauty of the young night forbade much apprehension in that direction.

From the intrusion of either man or beast everything was safe—of the latter the land was destitute, as has already been stated. Of the aborigines none were likely to intrude on that lonely spot, and if they did, what matter? they would not steal, and as to safety of life, why there was not a firearm amongst the whole party!

A lovely night succeeded what had been a lovely day. And such nights! Who can know their beauty and brilliancy but those who have seen them? The Southern Cross was brilliant in its beauty. There was no moon, but it was as light as it is at home when the moon is half at the full.

The Maoris sat around a blazing fire, variously occupied in the preparation of supper. The Pakehas were arranging the tent, spreading their beds of fern, of which a sufficient supply had already been brought to carpet the whole surface, and nothing could look more comfortable. A little lamp burned on the top of the big sea-chest which came out of the boat, and which served as a table for the coming supper, which was very soon afterwards partaken of in a very primitive manner. On the top of the chest was placed the inevitable three-legged gipsy pot, with the inevitable pork and potatoes inside it, and not far off were the inevitable tin pannikins with tea. Some woefully brown-looking sugar, some equally brown-looking ship's biscuit, such as was used in those days, and which Jack would turn his nose up at now, comprised the evening's banquet. But the supper was discussed with no small relish, and over it the plan for the morrow decided. We were to make the circut of the island in the canoe, and find out the best place to pitch the tent permanently, for on the morrow two of the three Pakehas were to be left to their own resources on the island, with the hound for company; while the other Pakeha, with his boat and Maori crew, proceeded still farther on their journey.

All was darkness now within the tent, and its curtain doors were drawn together, but Maori curiosity peering between them saw at the farther end of the tent two of the Pakehas endeavouring to court sleep; at the foot of the tent the Pakeha steersman was already in the arms of Morpheus, which arms the peeping Maoris wot not of!

The boat's crew then settled down comfortably around a blazing fire to thoroughly enjoy their pipes. Occasionally they heard a low murmuring in the tent, but the voices grew fainter and fainter; and to the two courters of sleep in the tent it appeared that the Maori fire blazed less and less brightly, and the soft Maori language fell softer and softer on their ears.

But the fire still blazed as brightly as ever; the Maori *korero* was not in less loud voice.

It was the sweet oblivion of sleep stealing over the travellers in their fern bed.

The fire flickered more and more—it went out. The voices died away—they ceased.

In reality the fire still burned brightly. The *korero* was still in audible voice.

But the two Pakeha wanderers from their far-off home

now lie tranquilly sleeping in their new home in the land of their adoption.

But the spirit of their dreams on this night hovered not over their fern couch nor under their tented roof, but travelled afar to their fatherland.

There they trod the mountain heath and explored the rocky glen, they gathered afresh the wild flowers and berries with the companions of their youth, they mingled once more in the sports of the field with the friends of their riper years, they lived over again many bygone days, bright and happy with the near and dear under the parental roof.

Ah! are there not as exquisite moments of happiness in our dreams as are ever enjoyed in our waking hours?

The Maoris no longer fed the fire; one by one they drew their mats around them, stretched themselves on the ground with but scanty sprinkling of fern underneath, and dropped asleep.

The hound moved closer to the tent-door and lay down so that no one could enter without stepping over him, and pillowing his head on his own body he too slept.

The night continued as serene as ever—not a breath of wind moved the leaves, now drinking the early dew-fall.

The stars shone down without a cloud to obscure their brilliancy, and were reflected from the smooth sea that girt the little island.

The ebbing waters receded from the gravelly shore without a ripple.

Not a sound, even the faintest, broke on the universal stillness.

All Nature slept.

And thus it was that the two Rangatira Pakehas of the good old Kanini took possession of their new home.

For had he not sold to them that lonely and far-away spot, the little island of Motu-Korea?

CHAPTER II

Monarchs of all they Surveyed : The Monarchs Turn Well-Sinkers

MORNING dawned as calmly and serenely as the preceding evening had sunk into night.

Daylight came struggling faintly and indistinctly into the tent when I awoke that morning from one long unbroken slumber.

I well remember—so vivid had been my dreams of home—that when I first awoke I could hardly realize that I lay on a bed of fern, but I thought that I must still be at home, and that my life since I left it was a dream from which I had not yet woke up.

But rub my eyes as I would I still saw the tented roof overhead, and the Maori language fell on my ear from without the tent, and the hound snuffing up the morning air stretched himself out with a yawning whine, and ended by giving a suppressed short bark, and putting his cold nose into my face, as if wishing me the most affectionate of greetings in my new home—which greeting he administered also to my still sleeping companion, and so awoke him.

'I suppose we *are* lying in a tent on a fern bed on the ground—that that is the sea out there—that this *is* Motu-Korea, our new home, though I have been dreaming of my old one so vividly that it has taken me some time to realize the true position of my life and precise time of its existence.'

It was thus I spoke, throwing off my blanket and jumping up.

'And I also would most certainly have believed I had awoke in "Auld Reekie", only no such pure air as this is to be had there, and one is not in the habit of having the cold nose of a dog pushed into one's face in one's bed in a civilized land, so I suppose I must confess to being really where I am, however difficult that very simple problem may be. I had better follow your example and get up, and as I do not hear any waves breaking on the beach, it will be a splendid morning for us to paddle round the island and examine all its nooks and corners in our canoe.'

On issuing from the tent we found the dawn fast chasing away all traces of night from the east, but to the west we still saw some lingering stars 'with lessening rays' shining 'to greet the early morn', ushering in the lovely day when Motu-Korea to us was born—that is a little bit of a travesty of Burns's loveliest of poems, but it reads naturally enough if it does not smack of true poetry.

The sky was cloudless, not a breath of air stirred, the reflection of the little mountain glassed itself in the smooth surface of the surrounding water.

The dew-scent rose fresh on all sides, for the vegetation around glistened with the pearly drops and seemed struggling through a crystal bath, so heavily lay the dew.

We might have washed ourselves in dew, but we were not quite nymphs, and were not enacting the poetry of life, so a tin basin, on a lump of scoria rock for a washstand, if neither poetical nor romantic, was much more practical and appropriate for the work we had before us.

Whilst our open-air toilet was being performed, the Maoris were launching the canoe for us into deep water, the tide having left it high and dry on the beach.

As we took our places in the canoe, Tartar—for the good old Kanini had given us the hound as a parting gift —scrambled in, and wished to make one of the party; but as he might, by jumping on the side, make the canoe rather unsteady for safe paddling, we dispensed with his company and made him jump out again. Seeing that the canoe skirted inshore, he scampered along the beach in close attendance.

In the course of a couple of hours we had made the complete circuit of our little sea-girt possession, and had explored every little bay.

We sat down on a scoria stone with a keen relish for our breakfast. Pork and potatoes never tasted better—tea was hardly wanted to wash down the meal. A good wholesome appetite, whetted by our morning's paddle, had also a relish given to it by the knowledge of what our morning's excursion had disclosed to us, for we were enchanted with all we had seen along the shore of the island, and we were in full hope that our inland exploration would confirm our first impression that we had fallen on quite a little prize, and that our new and lonely home would excel our fondest hopes and expectations.

After breakfast we saw Pama start in the boat with his crew bound on a visit to Wepiha's station at the Manukau. This mission from Waiomu, determined upon by Wepiha very soon after our arrival at Herekino, had been a very opportune one for us, as it afforded us the opportunity of crossing the gulf in the good new boat of Pama's building, which was large enough to take our canoe in tow, and thus bring us comfortably to the island. But though we had arrived safely we had not done so without having encountered some risk of losing our canoe.

The fact was, the boat was much too deeply laden, and a strong breeze blowing up the gulf, with a strong tide flowing down it, had raised such a 'jabble of a sea' that we ran some risk of being swamped, and we had to throw overboard some bags of salt, destined for Wepiha's station, to lighten the boat. We were very near being obliged to cast off the canoe, which, of course, became too heavy a drag in a sea-way.

Pama was to call again at the island in a day or two

on his way back to Herekino, and I promised to be ready
to accompany him part of the way. I was bound on a
small voyage down the inlet to present certain credentials
with which Kanini had armed us. They were addressed
to a sub-tribe, who were commanded to go to the island
and build his Pakehas a *whare*.

The letter was not an absolute command, but was in
reality equivalent to one, so I knew I was not starting on
a wild-goose chase without a certainty of being able to
get back to the island within a given time—always making due allowance for Maori *taihoa*-ism.

So we saw Pama pull away round the reef—the very
reef upon which Wepiha had bumped us in the dark that
night when a certain number of visionaries were town-
ship-site-hunting and came to grief, as it has been my
task to tell you.

How little did 'we twa' then think how well we
should come to know that reef, and how many would
be the dish of oysters we should gather off it!

Here, then, we were, with Tartar as company, all
alone in our glory to lord it over each other in our own
small dominion. In order to get a complete view of this
in a *coup d'œil* we at once determined to ascend our
little island's little mountain. A quarter of an hour's
rough scramble from the base, and we stood on its summit. We were not a little surprised to discover, *en route,*
signs that the island had once been inhabited. There were
long lines of stone walls here and there, and the usual
six-foot-high fern was replaced by a short dry-looking
grass—a sure sign that the land had been cropped for
many and many a year, so as to have completely eradi-
cated the fern. The sides of the hill were so thickly
covered with scoria that the fern was comparatively of
stunted growth.

As we approached the very summit, the scoria became
much smaller, redder, and burnt-looking, and on fairly
gaining the top all doubt of the island's volcanic origin
was set at rest, for we found an extinct crater at least a

hundred feet deep, its sides all round as regular in shape as a punch-bowl. The upper rim had a radius of some hundreds of yards. On the outer slope of the hill which we had traversed in our ascent we had crossed several well-defined terraces scooped out with great regularity, the lowest some fourteen feet in width, each higher one narrowing successively.

There was no doubt whatever that the island had been used as a stronghold and place of refuge in long-bygone days, and the terraces were the points of defence. In these later days, when the scrub and thick fern have given place to the bright green verdure of the grass which now covers the slopes of these volcanic hills, you can ride to the summits of many, and see extinct craters far surpassing in size that of little Motu-Korea, but none of more perfect form.

I am afraid the next forty years will do as little as the past forty years have done in throwing any light on the past history of the aboriginal people who actually terraced all those volcanic hills. Traditions there are of battles fought by some great chief, and the spots are localized by the names of volcanic mountains, but no thrilling tale is ever told of how one terrace after another was lost or gained, and the *pa* on the summit stormed.

I believe the generations of a far earlier race, one thickly populating the land and of whom we have no traditions whatever, were the artificers who scarped the vast works on those many mountains. The only record is a stray skull or two, the cranial development of which, compared with that of the Maori skull of the present day, shows as great a difference as between that of the Briton of to-day and that of the Briton of the days of Julius Cæsar. And the Briton of that day would not compare with the Maori of our day; they had only one feature in common, I think—both used war-paint!

As we walked round the crater margin we could survey, lying at our feet, the whole of our little sea-girt possession, and we were as proud of it as if it had been a small kingdom instead of a speck of an island of some hundred and fifty acres, for such proved to be its area.

We were surprised and delighted to find that there was a good deal of level land, for when passing the island it looked as if there were little save the crater-hill arising from the water. We now saw, however, that fine rich land lay all around the base of the hill, and quite a long level flat stretched away from one end towards the mainland.

Altogether it was a lovely place—pretty little bays were inclosed by picturesque headlands, all having some distinctive peculiarity. Then there arose from the level land near the base of the crater several little sugarloaf hills covered with rich brushwood. These hills could only have been formed by some immense shower of ashes vomited forth by the volcano, which, coming down vertically, had concentrated on one spot, forming these small pyramids.

One thing afforded us immense satisfaction—we saw a small pool of water in the centre of the level land. Old Kanini had told us of a spring on the eastern shore, but had not said anything about water in the centre of the island. The landscape from all points of view appeared to us as lovely then as it does now, and when you return with me to that far-off land, my children, you shall one day stand on the same spot and feast your own eyes on the landscape.

We saw Orakei Bay, and remembered our 'ragoût the Incomparable', and behind the bay arose Mount Remuera, from which we had first seen and coveted Motu-Korea, and now, behold! we stood on Mount Motu-Korea the owners of the soil, and our hopes were realised that we should pitch our tent on its shore and abide the wished-for event—the foundation of the capital of the colony by the Crown of Britain.

Descending from our 'high estate', we began exploring all the bays from the land point of inspection, having already done so by water, so as to determine the best locality in which to raise the roof-tree of our future home.

We finally fixed upon a spot with a snug little beach, protected on each side by a reef—very necessary for our canoe, for it was the most valuable of all our worldly possessions. From this spot, too, the mainland could be soonest reached, so we determined that here we would have our *whare* built—provided we succeeded in procuring water, for which we should be obliged to sink a well.

Water close at hand was the one thing abolutely indispensable, for we should require to act the beast of burthen *rôle* quite enough, without having to carry water to a distance from the spring, wherever we might find one. We should have to be our own hewers of wood, so the nearer we could do the drawing of water the better.

Having in our mind's eye fixed on the spot for the house, we there and then cleared away the brushwood and fern where we intended to begin sinking a well the first thing next morning. As we had our hatchets with us, it did not take us much time to do the small piece of clearing required. We then turned homewards to the tent, collecting as we walked along the beach a back-load of drift-wood, which was in due time deposited at the tent-door.

Sunset saw two great landed proprietors monarchs of all they surveyed—provided they did *not* look beyond the island itself—busy cooking their own dinner.

And that same day that Motu-Korea was born to them, the day that they walked from sunrise to sunset over their own broad acres, that day saw those great lords of the soil for the first time in their lives acting as their own cooks and getting their own dinner!

And in after-life they actually boasted of having arrived at this menial degradation!

Yes, they lived to see the day when the well appointed coal-merchant's wagon deposited the black diamonds of the colony's own production at villa residences where then grew fern and Nature reigned supreme—villa residences in the suburbs of the town they were then waiting

G

to see founded, whose locality even had not then been fixed upon.

Yes, they lived to see this, and ever recalled with pride and pleasure that first day when they were their own cooks in the little island of Motu-Korea!

Next morning 'we twa' had risen before the sun, and shaking the dew from off the brushwood as we pushed our way through it in going towards the well-site, we soon had our coats off, and went at it with a will as well-sinkers. We thought it wise to make the best of the cool of the morning for our new occupation; so, spell and spell about, we went at it, digging through one foot after another of beautiful rich volcanic soil, so that we began to wish with all our hearts it was not so deeply rich and would but change to clay to give us some hope of success.

Towards midday that rich soil gave no indication of coming to an end, so we beat a retreat to the reef close at hand, and as it was low water it had bared an immense oyster-field. We went at *that* now for a change, and made an onslaught to the tale of a terrible number could it only have been totted up—in fact, until we were almost as tired of eating oysters as we had been in trying to get through the volcanic soil in the well—that was never to be! For, alas! we dug, and we dug, until we had both to take a spell—strolling through the brushwood—and then another turn at the well, and then another turn at the oyster-bed; but the volcanic soil fairly got the best of us and drove us off discomfited.

At last the slanting rays of the setting sun, not down the well but aboveground, warned us we had certain culinary duties to undertake before sunset, and having gone through some twelve feet of soil with no indications of a change, we concluded that we must go farther and try to fare better by trying a new locality quite away from this rich flat and nearer the base of the hill.

If we had been disappointed in not getting water, *certes* we had not been so in finding a depth of rich soil, if that was any compensation.

And thus our second day was spent on the island.

The next morning we chose a much more beautiful spot for the house; it was charmingly picturesque, facing straight up the harbour, but there was no shelter on the beach in front for our canoe; but it would obviously be much better to have to go some distance when we wanted our canoe, which would be but seldom after all, than to have to fetch from a distance the ever-needed supply of water.

Good luck came to us on our second trial, for we found a break in the land quite a short distance behind the new site we had chosen for the house, and we had not sunk six feet before we came to a clay subsoil, and before the day was done we rejoiced in a well with water coming freely, and the next morning we awoke to find four feet of fine clear water—a supply which never gave out, and withstood all our household attempts to lessen the quantity.

On the afternoon of the following day Pama made his appearance from Orakei on his way back to Waiau, fulfilling his promise to call for me and land me at the Ngati Tai settlement at Umupuia.

So I had to leave Tartar to take care of his other master and the other master to take care of Tartar, and both of them to see that the island did not run away before I came back again.

This I promised to do with as much speed as was compatible with the take-it-easy and never-in-a-hurry character of Tangata Maori.

CHAPTER III

*I Present our Credentials to the Ngati Tai :
The Early Missionary*

I HAD no misgivings in leaving my brother-pioneer all
alone on the island; he would be just as safe there in
his solitary glory with Tartar as I should be all alone in
the midst of the strange tribe to whom I was bound. He
had no more firearms than I had, but he certainly had a
large stock of ammunition with which he could fight any
number of natives likely to come his way. I too had
armed myself with like munitions, my cartouche-box
being filled with tobacco cartridges.

With half a fig of tobacco any native appearing on the
scene of action could be shot off (if not finally disposed
of) at all events until that shot from that locker was
smoked out, when perhaps a return of the tobacco fight
might come off—a fight of words only.

On the evening of the same afternoon that I left
the island I was landed at the other end of the inlet at
my place of destination, Umupuia, by Pama, and he proceeded home to Waiau.

My letter of credentials from Kanini to Te Tara, head
chief of the Ngati Tai, was received by him with every
sign of high respect for the quarter from which it proceeded, and I was immediately made much of.

Te Tara appointed his own wife—he had only one,
having been converted from his ways of polygamy—to
be my handmaiden and attend upon me. The hand-

maiden being a rather ancient party, and mother of a grown and growing-up family, I was safe from falling an untimely victim to her charms.

The largest *whare* in the village was swept and garnished with clean fern for me. No one had to vacate the premises, for it was the meeting-house which had arisen when Te Tara forswore his extra wives and turned *mihinare,* was converted from his heathen ways, and took to psalm-singing at the solicitation of his reverend converter.

During my sojourn, however, at Umupuia, this big *whare* became occupied by all the personages of importance, male and female, irrespective of age, of the tribe, to do their smoking and gossiping *korero*-ing, not a few making it their sleeping quarters as well.

The nice clean fern covered the earthen floor; then a new clean mat was spread upon it for *me,* and a good many not nice clean ones were also spread on either side of mine, which told me I was not going to be without company.

By the time these preparations were made I had heard my letter of introduction read a dozen times, for every new-comer who kept dropping in from the *kumara* plantations had the benefit of the composition.

Such a great arrival, a live Rangatira Pakeha bringing such a letter, did not happen every day at Umupuia; no, indeed! this was the first occasion of the kind, so little wonder the most was made of it.

Before dark I found myself comfortably stretched full length on my mat, and large as was the *whare,* it was as full as it could hold of the tribe gentle and simple, all in the most intense state of gratification that they had got hold of a Rangatira Pakeha to smoke and talk over. Although I hated tobacco-smoke above all things, I had to suffer and be strong and minister to my own discomfort by distributing gifts of the, to me, noxious weed to my new friends to make them happy in the possession of their pipes of peace.

As the evening went on denser and denser grew the smoke, which kept pouring out in volumes from all around me until I was fain to lie down flat on my back to get my head as low as possible to avoid gulping down solid mouthfuls, for there *was* a space of about two feet high from the ground which was free from it. Heaven knows, I felt myself utterly unable to hold a high head that night amongst my new friends. I made occasional rushes out into the open air to breathe more freely for a few minutes and cool myself down, for the *whare* was intensely warm, a large fire blazing away in the centre of the floor, surrounded by old and young, and pipes here, pipes there, and pipes everywhere in fullest swing.

Ah, did I not envy the solitary occupant of the snug little tent on Motu-Korea?

The infliction lasted the whole night. I got snatches of sleep, but it mattered not when I awoke, I saw a knot of smokers round the fire hard at work. I heard them talking about Kanini, Waiomu, Motu-Korea, *te whare, te* Pakeha, and *utu*—this last word, 'payment', being the burthen of their song. To that one word I fell asleep; to that one word I woke again; sleeping or waking *utu* it was—*utu* evermore.

But I had one reflection to comfort me during this small purgatory I was undergoing. Te Tara had consented to come with his people to Motu-Korea to build us a *whare,* so I could well afford to allow them to discuss in anticipation the *utu* they would receive for building it.

Oh! how I wished that night that I could have loved tobacco as they did, and smoked a pipe myself! But it was never vouchsafed to me, neither then nor throughout my life, to smoke the pipe of consolation. I hate tobacco now even as I did then; more was the pity then!

But how remiss I have been! I have failed to chronicle at its proper time, shortly after sundown when I took possession of my quarters, a circumstance which would have rejoiced the hearts of all subscribers to Exeter Hall in general and Foreign Missions in particular. As the sun dipped behind the distant hills an old woman could be seen holding in one hand a three-legged pot, suspended by a blade of flax, which she struck with a stone held in the other hand, and thus tolled a chime which called the tribe to evening prayers.

The *whare* filled immediately with devout worshippers, who, muffled in their mats and blankets, strewed themselves over the floor in a promiscuous manner. The conductor of the religious ceremony then gave out a psalm, upon which all assembled forthwith gave out in song what I supposed to be some Pakeha tune which doubtless the *mihinare* had endeavoured to teach them.

But alas for the extraordinary noise that fell upon my ear! I utterly failed to recognize it, or from what tune it was a falling away. The imitation was not to be traced to any tune religious or profane—in fact, the sound was quite terrible, even in the low suppressed tone in which —fortunately for me—it was given. It had nothing either European or Maori about it; of the former element the instructing Missionary had utterly failed to impart any resemblance. If it had only been allowed to assume the latter, any Maori lament and chant or song, save the war song, would have been better than the hideous incongruity into which the ill-used psalm tune had drifted.

It was, however, decorously given, and after it a chapter from the New Testament was read, winding up with the Lord's Prayer—all in the Maori language, of course. Even at that date the Scriptures had been translated into Maori, and were in the hands of the missionaries for distribution.

On the Amen being pronounced the whole meeting-house, as if by a stroke of an enchanter's wand, was instantaneously converted into a gossiping hall again, with accompanying incense proceeding from innumerable pipes, all hard at work before the parson had stuck his Testament behind one of the rafters overhead—a sort of depôt for storing away things.

'Ah! how beautiful for this simple, untutored race to

assemble thus night and morning in their own rude way to worship the Lord!' I can imagine the dear old ladies of Exeter Hall exclaiming; and I can also, without any very great stretch of imagination, conjure up the touching and telling picture a returned Missionary could paint when addressing an Exeter Hall audience, taking for his text 'The Umupuia Maoris at prayer'.

But, dear ladies, a word in your ear—just a little word in your ear. Do you suppose the Maori understands what he has been—parrot-fashion—repeating, or that he can in any way enter into and appreciate the pure spirit of Divine revelation? Alas, dear ladies, I must despoil you of the ecstatic belief in which you have been erroneously revelling! It is a mere delusion by which both the Missionary and Exeter Hall are deluded, and I would that I might allow you to hug this belief to your religious hearts in peace; but my conscience forbids it.

I hold the countless thousands spent in converting the heathen to be truly 'a vain thing'; they ought to be spent nearer home—surely charity ought to begin there. Who shall say there are not heathen steeped in deepest ignorance of Christianity within the chime of Bow Bells in the modern Babylon?

But, alas! no *éclat* would arise from missionary conversion in that quarter—no excitement to fill Exeter Hall and extract subscriptions. Yet too certainly could thrilling tales be told of deepest human degradation, but what romance could there be drawn from that source of supply? How much pleasanter *not* to hear of it—to keep it away deep down out of sight and revealing!

But a sentimental story from a far-off land under a sunny sky, of how savages who once had been given to eating each other now tolled the bell—what though it were only a three-legged pot—to morning and evening prayer on Umupuia shore! Ah! that was pleasant to listen to, a halo of romance enshrined a narrative drawn from that source. These were not disagreeable naked truths speaking home to the heart unpleasantly because too true

—truths which it is a foul disgrace to have existing in our very midst—a disgrace which no conscience dare deny, but which is shut out of sight and relegated to an unrevealed future.

How supremely grotesque was ever the Exeter Hall romance tale of conversions when compared with the Antipodean reality as known to the pioneer settlers! But how could it have been otherwise?

The early missionaries who came in contact with the Maori race (with one or two bright exceptions, whom I delight to honour) were not men who could command respect or even cope with the 'savage faculty' in intellect. I wish not to be misunderstood in the remarks I am about to pass (made in sorrow, not ridicule) on the humble but brave men who went with their lives in their hands to live amid a savage but highly-intellectual race to convert them to religion *and teach them a trade*. It was a fatal error to suppose that men with this double qualification would prove the right men in the right place amongst such a highly-intelligent race as the Maoris. The trade they might have taught them, but the grafting of religion on to it was the tacking on of mental work of which they were incapable, save by the rule of rote. The selection, perforce, was given to the missionary who had followed a trade and could teach *it*, and if he were willing to face the conversion of the heathen, the capability to do so was taken for granted. But no greater mistake was ever made. When respect for mental capacity of the teacher is wanting, small is the effect of the doctrines inculcated, in the mind of the taught.

Such, in a word, was the state of the case between the early Missionary and the Maori. Kanini's little trip-up of the converting Missionary, when he told him there could be no 'casting into outer *darkness*' when 'fire and brimstone' were hard at work, was but a little side-play compared to the strong reasoning with which he could have coped with his adversary.

The Missionary teacher in his own mechanical way—

which caused his selection for his work—would have been convincingly overwhelming. He could have rattled his wheelwright's hammer about old Kanini's ears and flashed his chisel before his eyes in a way which would most infallibly have convinced the chief that *Te Mihinare* was the better man of the two—at that work! Kanini would have felt a strong conviction that it was but a mere matter of time before he, too, would be able to make wheeled vehicles strong enough to carry his whole tribe, laden with their ancient superstitious *tapu* and all, over the roughest road to Christian conversion—could the missionary but have shown him *that* path.

But that was just what the missionary could not do. He had taught his pupils to read and write their own language in our characters—for no Maori one ever existed —he had taught them the reading of the Scriptures by rule, and the saying of prayers by rote, and the singing of hymns to a hideously discordant noise, but to these outward forms of worship no inward feelings of conviction had been added. It was mere word-worship, not heart-devotion—a mere substitute of *one kind of superstition for another* in Maori eyes.

Very sad this, my dear ladies of Exeter Hall—sad, but none the less true.

I promised the proof some chapters back, and I shall now give it you.

Five years later than the date of which I now write (which period I throw in to Exeter Hall to allow the Maori a still longer time to become properly imbued with the proper appreciation of the religion to which they had been—outwardly—converted)—five years later, when the chief Heke stood arrayed in hostile attitude against the Government, but *not* the settlers, and when Nene took up the quarrel and fought for us until Her Majesty's troops could take the field, our native allies included both converted and unconverted tribes. One morning, before going forth to do battle, two priests, a heathen and a missionary, were offering prayers side by side for success to their arms, *each performing their respective parts*—I use this language designedly—the heathen priest his incantation; the converted priest the Lord's Prayer. The first sentence only of the latter had been repeated, when, suddenly stopping, the missionary turned to the incantation-man and said, *'Now take care and don't make a mistake in your part, and I won't make a mistake in mine!'*

In mine?

In his what? Oh! Exeter Hall?

A Christian *prayer?*

Can you call it such?

I cannot; the word I am constrained to use is simply—incantation.

And it is for such conversion England spends her countless thousands—alas!

Oh! ladies of Exeter Hall, why look you not nearer home? Have you no bowels of compassion for your own sex who are daily driven by cruel starvation beyond the reclaiming aid of any missionary, who sell both body and soul for the means of subsistence, dragging through a living death, and you might assuage their sufferings and save their souls from perdition?

But you will not.

'Convert the heathen!' is your motto—not the heathen at your own door, more numerous than in all the isles of Polynesia—but the heathen basking in the sunny climes of far-off lands, the heathen bountifully supplied by Nature's prodigal hand.

Oh! ye Foreign Missions that only make your heathen change one form of incantation for another, and that so miserably fail to imbue your converts with any true idea of the guiding principle of Christian faith, I pray ye stay at home.

NOTE: Since these lines were penned many years have passed, but have only too truly and painfully proved that the missionary teaching resulted in nought but substituting one outward form of worship for another. And what resulted, even after one great master-mind followed in the wake of the simple early missionary, and took up the 'good work'. (I believe that is the accepted and proper phrase to use)? The Maori wars only chronicled in painful characters of blood, the utter failure of all missionary labour when the newly-converted tribes fell away from the Christian faith—faith indeed!—and invented new faiths of their own and ran riot in them.

Yes, even the teaching of Selwyn failed to leave any impress; and after many years, and in his own day and time, he had to weep to see the heartrending collapse of his great labour.

And if *his* great grasp of mind and character, imbued with such a generous and chivalrous devotion to the Maori race, whose motto indeed was Maoriland for the Maoris— if his indomitable zeal failed to instil true religion into the native mind, how could the simple primitive 'mechanic missionary' ever have succeeded?

CHAPTER IV

I Learn what Taihoa Means

MY patience was tested by a three-days' residence at at the Umupuia gossiping-hall. And well it earned that name before Te Tara and his followers had fitted out and equipped their largest canoe to take me and themselves back to my island home to build the *whare* that was to be that home. But at length a start was made, and I congratulated myself that I should sleep that night under the canvas roof of the little tent in Motu-Korea.

But I never made a greater miscalculation in my life. I had yet to learn the true meaning of that Maori word *'taihoa'* which was doomed to be as indelibly graven on my memory as the word *utu* had already been during my stay at the village upon which I was now thankfully turning my back. Of the meaning of *taihoa* I had a vague dread from the small experiences I had already passed through, but I was about to be awakened to a true valuation of the power of that word which can be so fearfully and wonderfully exercised by Tangata Maori.

We had no sooner rounded Umupuia Point than we opened the inlet, and there away at its other extremity lay the little island, raising its little mountain aloft as if beckoning to me and welcoming me home again.

But we had hardly faced towards it and paddled along for more than ten minutes, when suddenly, upon passing another point of land, we steered right in shore—we were creeping close along it—and before I could ask why we were going in here the canoe had already reached the beach and become emptied of its paddlers as if by magic.

The *haeremai* and *tautimai* ('come', and 'come to my arms') of some blanketed figures standing near some huts seemed to exercise the most uncontrollable influence over my friends, and before I had got out of the canoe and recovered from my surprise I saw quite a brisk nose-rubbing being performed.

I strolled up to the group, thinking I should discover the reason why we had stopped here, but on coming within earshot I beat an immediate retreat. I arrived just in time to hear the commencement of the narrative of my arrival at Umupuia, with the Kanini letter of introduction, which was being produced and read to greedy ears. And I knew all that was to follow—I had said this and that and the other thing, and I had washed my face and hands absolutely twice a day, when I got up and when I went to bed, that I did not smoke tobacco, which always provoked an exclamation of extreme surprise—in fact, almost every word spoken and every act performed by this newly-caught Pakeha was faithfully set down and retailed over again.

I had listened to this blessed repetition at Umupuia after every arrival of any intruder who had come to the village until I was sick at heart of this too-oft-repeated tale, but I now awoke to the hideous conviction that I had not yet passed out of this small purgatory and I had still to suffer.

To mitigate the future sufferings which I now clearly saw awaited me, I registered a vow in confidence to myself that I would not open my mouth again except to say 'yes' and 'no', and put *kumara* into it. For I had discovered that the ever-repeated narrative grew longer and longer, and even as anything more had been said by me, so did it become tacked on to the story which had to be told to every new friend encountered.

'But when, when, when shall we be at Motu-Korea?' was my appeal half-a-dozen times each day.

'*Taihoa, taihoa, taihoa*', was ever the answer, drawled out in the most inimitable and imperturbably good-humoured voice, each *taihoa* longer than the one before.

'Oh damn *taihoa*!' was the *not* imperturbable or good-humoured reply which did *not* fall upon Maori ears, for I ground it out between my teeth in such *sotto voce* that if relief came to me from the anathema, no harm fell upon my listener.

For six mortal days had I to succumb to *taihoa*!

I am free to confess I got through an amount of anathematizing during those six days, totting up such a big account, that I am persuaded that if all the swearing of my after-life was put against it in an opposite column the *taihoa* one would carry the day.

Not a hamlet of half-a-dozen *whares* on the shore as we skirted along—the longed-for haven of the little island ever in sight—but the nose of the canoe was poked into the beach. In vain my protestations. '*Taihoa, taihoa,* all in good time—what's the hurry, O Pakeha!' time was made for slaves—hurry no man's cattle, as we in the classics say. 'What's the odds, a day or two sooner or later? There's Motu-Korea; it won't run away—*taihoa nei*?' with a chuck back of the head as they ended with the interrogative. I declare there never was invented a more aggravating situation than having to stand calmly and listen to the *taihoa* extinguisher with the intensely good-natured concluding *nei*? I remember thinking that their heads could not be screwed on the right way, and wishing they had been, when probably they might have lost their temper with me, and that would have been such a chance to return the compliment and blow off one's pent-up steam of confined passion in a grand explosion, and my poor weak human nature—as compared to that of Tangata Maori—would have been relieved.

But I smothered it all down, and it came about that I rivalled Job himself, and inwardly congratulated myself that I had quite taken the shine out of that ancient patriarch and made him look quite small.

At last, however, the *più tarde* of this *dolce far niente* race was exchanged for the *subito*. *Taihoa* was replaced by *'aianei'* (directly); they were now going to be at the island directly, if not sooner. The fact was they had exhausted every little bay and creek where dwelt even one solitary and half-toothless old woman in whom could be found a listener to the story they had to tell. How I had envied Canning's needy knife-grinder—'Story, sir! I have none to tell!'

Hurrah! round the last point of land—the island in sight again; we have been buried away down a deep bay, the island again almost within grasp; now we shoot past the plumed headland of old acquaintance. The crew, one and all, male and female and children, make a dash at the finish; in full paddling-chorus chant they send the water flying from their paddles, and, oh marvel! I have succeeded in performing a three-hours' easy paddle from Umupuia to the island in just exactly twice as many days.

Great is the power of *taihoa!*

The canoe-song had, of course, warned the island's solitary occupant that we were at hand, and he had time to walk from the tent to the end of the beach before the canoe arrived.

'Did you think I had been put into a Maori *hangi* (native oven) and taken out again to grace a native feast?' I said on jumping ashore.

'No, wasn't the least afraid—no danger of a man being eaten who is destined to meet another more exalted fate. But, joking apart, what in the name of wonder has kept you? More than once, when I was having a look-out for you from the top of the hill, I saw the canoe crawling along in shore.'

'Kept me! Nothing but that damned *taihoa* kept me— might have been here five days and nine hours ago. It is just six since we started. Don't I wish you had been in my place, that's all? By Jove! I'll give *you* the benefit next time anything of the kind is going on. Your small organ of combativeness is eminently more fitted to cope with *taihoa* than mine. Why I have done more quiet swearing than would serve for the whole natural term of my life. I positively am afraid my angelic temper has been next thing to ruined, and may never re-assert itself—in which case I pity you.'

'*E hoa, tena koe*', said Te Tara, putting out his hand to be shaken by his new Pakeha friend.

This greeting put an end to my tale of woe and how I had been forced to put Job to shame, and I did not get my oar in again to dilate on the subject until the tent-door closed upon us that evening.

We had no difficulty in coming to an understanding with Te Tara and his people with regard to the building of our *whare*. We staked off the dimensions on the actual site, put a sapling in the ground to show the height the walls were to be, marked out the passage and the two rooms on each side, specified the number of layers of *raupo* (sedge) that were to be put on the walls, and the description of thatching to be used, and the time within which the work was to be finished. A time non-fulfilment penalty was a thing utterly unknown in Maori contracts: the *taihoa* Maori mind simply could not have understood what it meant. We had no fear but that the house would be duly erected according to agreement in every respect except one, but with regard to that one the experience of my six-days' journey to accomplish three-hours' paddling raised such an infinitely knotty problem for solution, that I already sighed the sigh and actually groaned the groan of a misplaced confidence in the Maori assertion as to the three weeks in which the *whare* was to be finished, and I threw myself hopefully and trustfully into the arms of Providence, exclaiming, '*Taihoa,* we'll see!'

We thought, however, that the house would be finished some time or other; for, once begun, our friends would not go away until they got their *utu* for building it, and we also knew they would only get the *utu* when we gave it to them—as to their *taking* a dollar's-worth unless *given* by us, the idea never entered into our heads;

not one of them would take even a *'puru'* of tobacco to fill one pipe however much they longed for it; our whole possessions might lie exposed at their mercy, but not a pin's head would be touched. Having got from us the details of the work which they had to do, they held a long *korero* together, and then they handed us a *written* list—I thank thee, O missionary! for *that* teaching—of what they required as *utu*. This consisted of blankets, cotton print, calico, shirts, trousers (they were already imbibing civilized ideas, and believed civilization commenced in clothing their nether extremities), cloth caps, spades, hatchets and of course the inevitable and dearly-loved pipes and ambrosial weed.

The sum total represented some £15. We signed the *utu* list to show we agreed to the demand made, and handed it back to Te Tara, both contracting parties equally pleased with the bargain made.

And thus it was that we arranged that the roof-tree of our new home on our little island was to be raised to cover a mansion of the noble proportions of thirty feet by twenty-four, a grand corridor down the centre opening into four grand apartments. Grand!—of course they were. Why any one of them could hold our tent—six feet by eight! Everything is by comparison in this world! But 'we twa' had no intention of leaving our Maori friends to be the sole builders at work, for we had drawn upon our architectural capabilities in designing yet another building, which was to be erected a stone's throw from the mansion, and which, moreover, was to be a thoroughly substantial stone building—at all events we were quite satisfied the stones would be quite substantial whatever else was not. The structure was to be scoria and 'dab'. We had abundance of scoria all around, and the dab was also not far off—that is, the material from which it was made, for the clay we had dug out of our well, with a proper application of water, would enable us to puddle the two together to the proper consistency to make our 'dab' with which to rear the scoria walls for our cookhouse.

We now removed the tent from the eastern shore, where we had pitched it the first night of our arrival, to the opposite or western shore, close beside where our *whare* was to be put up, and handy to our well, so that we should have an eye to the building going up by the Maoris, and be close to our own work as well.

The natives soon ran up some breakwind huts for themselves, and then they made trips to the mainland to provide the necessary materials for our *whare,* and it was not long before they had all the upright poles which constituted the walls stuck in the ground and the framework formed.

The Pakehas divided their time between 'scoria and dab' and making a small garden, for no time was to be lost in planting such seeds as we had, however roughly put into the ground—potatoes, pumpkins, rock and water melons constituted our stock and store; of other seeds we had none.

Our friends made a great spurt at the first starting, and then they began to hang fire; they had coaxed us out of some tobacco in advance, and though the *whare* hung fire, it was more than their pipes did. Had they shown the same assiduity in *raupo*-ing the walls of the house as they did in smoking their pipes we should have had no cause to grumble, but many pipes meant much *taihoa,* and we began to look with sinister eye on the manner in which the play was now being acted.

Of course we spurred them on and began asking them *when* they would be finished, and of course we got the imperturbable *taihoa* given to us with the customary placid good-humour—*taihoa* and nothing more, just as if we had asked the question for the first time.

It is my opinion that half the evil deeds in the world would never be committed if all nations that on earth do dwell had only been providentially blessed by having in their language that potent word—*taihoa!*

CHAPTER V

Waiting in Expectancy

TAIHOA had now killed off the three weeks in which the house was to have been finished, and it was little more than half-finished. And so it came about that our little garden gave forth quite refreshing green signs of life, and we began to have misgivings that the very potatoes we had planted might, by the virtue of *taihoa*-ism, be ready to dig before the dining-room was finished in which we hoped to have eaten them.

And we began to wax impatient—very, for we wanted to have the house out of hand so that we could then get Te Tara to take us in his large canoe across the Hauraki to Herekino, for we craved to see Wepiha and learn some news of the outer world.

It was now some six weeks since we had communication with our fellow-Pakehas in the land, and we began to wonder what had transpired about the movements of the Government and the capital—where *was* it to be fixed?

Te Tara had given us a half-promise to take us, but upon our pushing him home on the point, and asking him to make a start, he caved in and declined. The fact was he was afraid to go, for although the Maori tribes were then at peace, still in the days of which I write there existed amongst them a strong mistrust of each other, and the Ngati Tai being but a very small tribe, it would not have created any very great sensation if they had all been eaten off the face of Maoridom.

So our friends deemed prudence the better part of valour, and preferred staying where they were in the *flesh* to running the risk of being converted into that article for foreign consumption, and only living in the *spirit*.

So *taihoa* did yet greatly prevail, and great was the dawdling over the *whare*.

We grew so hungry for some news of the outer world that we seriously meditated an attempt to paddle across the firth in our little canoe. But we should have been obliged to wait for a calm day before venturing, so we ultimately caved in, even as Te Tara had done, and acted the prudent part, and had to be content to do *taihoa* as to finding our way to see Wepiha at Herekino.

Taihoa got so completely the best of it that while we were waiting our potatoes and pumpkins and melons all made their appearance, carpeting the ground and show-ing great promise of not far-distant prolific results. And our cookhouse was finished and 'dabbed' to completion before the mansion was finished, though even in spite of the length of the *taihoa* that the natives took, that even approached almost to completion.

And all these great improvements were good and pleasant to behold, yet they satisfied us not. Many would have rejoiced over such a life 'devoid of care', but that figure of speech means something very akin to stagna-tion, and makes one think of lying on the flat of the back basking in the sun, and dropping macaroni into one's mouth under an Italian sky. And life devoid of care is not the motto on the banner which leads onward. It was not in us to lie basking on the sunny shore of Motu-Korea and make the Maori *taihoa* the burthen of our song.

There was to be a future for Maoriland under the Pakeha, and we were craving to know when the first page of its history was to be written—query, was it not so already? And so we unkindly denounced the Ngati Tai as very stupid and tiresome at being frightened to paddle us over to Herekino, though we admitted they were very good fellows for coming to build us a house.

But relief came when we least looked for it, for one day we heard the exclamation from a thatcher busy on the roof of the *whare, 'Te Pakeha e haeremai—te poti e haeremai!'* So we sang out, 'Hurrah! news at last!' Yes, news at last, for here was Pama coming, so we were saved the risk of drowning ourselves *en route* to Herekino had we gone in our own canoe, and the Ngatí Tai were saved the risk of being eaten had they taken compassion upon us and taken us in theirs.

Pama had brought us a welcome supply of 'trade', which was the term then used to mean a stock of goods adapted for trading with the natives—which we had ordered from Sydney, and which had arrived to Wepiha's care. We were now in a position to pay all our debts—the old Kanini for the island, Te Tara for building our *whare,* and we had now the means of buying the necessaries of life in the shape of pigs and potatoes whenever considerate aborigines visited us with intent to barter. The island, however, was not as yet lying in the great thoroughfare of commerce, for we had to tell Pama that we had never seen one single canoe, far less a boat, pass it since the day we had landed.

But Pama brought us startling and cheering news, of a kind which promised ere long to rob our little sea-girt possession of any claim to being a solitary place, and far from the haunts of men, for it was soon to lie on the very threshold of a future populous neighbourhood.

The Government had discovered the harbour of the Waitemata, and the capital was to be built upon its shores.

'We twa' shouted a wild hurrah when this welcome news fell upon our ears, and we began acting something like the 'Hielan' fling', and if we did not hug Pama it was only because we were afraid the Maori lookers-on might think we were seized with some cannibal intent towards our countryman and pay us a similar compliment.

Yes, the panorama from the crater-summit of Remuera had been gazed upon by other eyes than ours since we had stood on that spot last autumn. The governor of the colony had stood there, and it now and for evermore became known to Pakehas as Mount Hobson. He had looked down upon the isthmus, stretching from sea to sea, and only the question of whether the new capital should be higher up or lower down the Waitemata remained to be decided.

When we were busy digging out our canoe in the forest of Waiomu we little thought our anticipations regarding the future of the isthmus were to be so speedily realised. While we were at work a survey cutter had been lying quietly at anchor in the Waitemata and a survey of the harbour had been completed; and Pama went the length of saying that the very spot on which the future capital was to be built was already fixed, and that no long time would elapse before the plan of the town would be commenced, for the land had been already purchased from the Ngati Whatua.

I suppose there had not been any squabble over the fag-end of a potful of soup, and Te Hira had not been in the sulks, and the very land which we had wanted to purchase for 'the town that never was' now belonged to the Government. And so it turned out that Te Hira's sulks had been a fortunate thing for township-site-hunters, for had they dealt with the natives for the land they would only have got into a squabble with the Government, and certainly would have gone to the wall.

Pama was going to the Te Hira settlement, so in a day or two, on his return, we should get all the news from the Maori fountain-head—from the actual sellers of the land.

The next time 'we twa' passed round the crater-edge, on the summit of our island, how bouyant was our step, and what an enhanced value our little domain had acquired in our eyes!

Great was the suspense in which we were kept until

Pama's return, and great the disappointment he brought to us, for we had been discounting the situation too prematurely, and had a sudden come-down from our high hopes.

Yes, alas! the Ngati Whatua knew nothing whatever about the capital; no purchase of land had been made; *they* knew nothing of where the Pakeha town was to be.

What they did know was only this: A small vessel had come into the Waitemata, that Pakehas had landed at Orakei and gone to the top of Remuera, and that they had gone away again after sailing all round the harbour; that afterwards another smaller vessel had come, and had kept sailing all round about and through the harbour, and a small boat had pulled into all the bays, and that a long time had been spent doing this, and then one morning the vessel was no more to be seen; but as the natives had all been away at Mangere *kumara*-planting and shark-fishing, this was all they knew, gathered from an old woman left at the Orakei settlement.

And so we had to conclude it was very much like the old story of one's neighbour settling all one's business and knowing all about it better than one's self, and we were left to draw what conclusions we chose as to the 'capital to be'.

So we discounted our new situation to the following conclusion: That the 'capital' question had faded away towards the end of the year; that we must be up and doing and not *taihoa*-ing and letting the fern grow under our feet; that the only one thing we could do was to stock our island with the only edible animal that existed in the land, and which, of course, would be in demand as soon as there was a capital and citizens to inhabit it, who would require supplies of daily food.

So we determined to convert the island into a pig-station—make a pig-run of it; and in due course of time we might look forward to being able to paddle our own canoe, with our own reared pigs, to a 'capital' market somewhere, we hoped, in sight of our own island.

We told Pama, on his return to Waiau, to send a message to a certain Pakeha who owned a small undecked schooner to find his way to Motu-Korea, as we wanted him on a pig-purchasing expedition; and so away went Pama.

Our mansion was now approaching completion, and only wanted the second coat of *raupo* lining, when one day a canoe arrived with a message that the Ngati Tai must put in an appearance somewhere or other at a '*tangi*'. Some stupid old woman had gone to explore the Maori bourn, and had to be duly *tangi*'d over.

This summons was imperative; the rapidity with which our friends bundled their traps and themselves into their canoe was enough to make anyone believe they had forever forsworn *taihoa,* and expunged the word from their language. They made such precipitate 'tracks' that we could only get one word out of them when we anxiously demanded when they would be back to finish their work, and that one word, what could it be but— '*Taihoa*'?

And that *taihoa* remained *taihoa* for evermore.

They never came back to finish the house, and it never was finished.

Strange events happened that caused us never to require that that house should be finished, and it never was either by us or anyone else.

We had hoped to have got hold of a Ngati Tai boy to remain with us and do our hewing of wood and drawing of water for us, but it was no go, they all would go; one was going to have the initiatory tattooing of one side of his nose begun, another was going to have the tattooing of the other side of his nose finished, and so we were left all alone to get on as best we could, to collect our own drift-wood, to draw our own water, and practically test of what mettle we were made, and to what account we could turn the cookhouse we had ourselves built, and of which we were ourselves to be the cooks!

CHAPTER VI

My Maiden Venture in the Field of Commerce

THAT old 'Pakeha Maori'—the name by which such of our countrymen as married Maori maidens and became half-Maoris were known—had evidently been doing his good share of *taihoa* since we sent for him to come to the island, for we strained our eyes in vain down the inlet to see the white sails of his schooner making alive the solitary though lovely stretch of water; but we looked in vain.

And so we grew impatient exceedingly, and neither the carrying home of drift-wood on our backs, nor the drawing of water from the well, nor the great feats we performed in the culinary art in our cookhouse, sufficed to content us and keep the demon of discontent from our *whare* door.

For we were killing the present, and were awaiting with eager anxiety that future which we hoped would dawn upon us with such bright prospects, but as yet there was no break of day, and we were both young, and youth is ever impatient.

And our impatience had been increased by our having one day seen a small topsail schooner round the north head of the harbour and steer straight across to Orakei Bay, and lie there until sunset with unfurled sails; but next morning the strange craft was not there.

Then, again, we had seen the same craft pay a second

and still shorter visit about ten days later, and on this occasion she did not even anchor, but only stood off and on the bay, whilst her boat went ashore and returned, when away the vessel sailed again.

Now it was this visitor that had so roused our curiosity and made us discontented, for we were firmly convinced this topsail schooner could only have come from Kororareka, where the Government was then located, and we believed it had something to do with the future capital, and at this epoch of our Robinson Crusoe life in our little island we were suffering from a most persistent and continued attack of 'capital on the brain'.

We should have taken our canoe and paddled up to the Orakei settlement, only every hour we expected our Pakeha Maori to turn up with his small craft, the *Dart,* in which I was about to make my maiden venture in the domain of commerce. In this trip I should come in contact with the Ngati Whatua and be able to learn all that was known about the topsail schooner.

When at last the *Dart* arrived, she did not come careering swiftly o'er the water like a thing of life, but, belying her name, crawled one morning slowly into sight, and, though she had been lazy in making her appearance, still the little tub was very welcome.

We got news from that late seat of kingly power, Herekino; it had lapsed into its primitive state of Pakeha-Maoridom, and Wepiha was no longer a king, but only Taniwha's white man, married to his daughter. Great had been his fall, and ere long the commerce of Te Hauraki would be transferred from Waiau to Waitemata. His oracular utterance of 'Wait till you see the Waitemata', which was to make those who heard him, figuratively speaking, fall down and worship her shores, had not been spoken in vain, nor without a presentiment that the harbour he so eulogised might one day be the seat of a great commerce, and little Waiau fade into significance.

The little tub *Dart* had her sails loose, all ready, waiting for the supercargo to go on board, and I (little more than a beardless boy, as ignorant of the ways of commerce as any green youth who had never seen life beyond the learned walls of his university from which he took his M.D. degree could be) was going to act an entirely new *rôle,* and transmogrify·the 'experienced surgeon', late of the *Palmyra,* into supercargo of the tub *Dart,* starting on a trading voyage!

There is but a step from the sublime to the ridiculous. Supercargo is sometimes a grand title, to be supercargo of an Indiaman 1,000 tons burthen, A 1, with from ten to fifty thousand pounds' worth of merchandise to barter for gold, ivory, and spices, *is* grand; but to be supercargo of the tub *Dart*—not A 1 by any means, and only 10 tons burthen, and with some 'trade', only worth two or three ten-pound notes, which we intended to barter for some pigs, possibly a stray goat or two, and the wherewithal in shape of potatoes and maize to store the cookhouse and keep body and soul together—well, it *was* very small rain on the tender herb of our budding commerce!

But what would you? Was the A1 1,000-tonner built in a day? Were the tens of thousands of money made in a week? Were not grand merchants once—said I in confidence to myself as I discounted my situation—were they not once small merchants?

And why should not I, then, the supercargo of small wares, have a grand future?

And so I dreamed my happy dream of youth, far away into future days, and was comforted.

Ah! in looking back—now so long, long back—to those days buried in the past, to those days of pioneer struggles, never to be erased from the tablets of one's memory, with what a halo of romance, notwithstanding all that was then encountered, is the remembrance surrounded now that youth's brightest dreams have been far more than realized!

'Tis so easy now to set down sapient reflections—to wit, it is no use for a young man to sit down with his hands before him, and say, 'It is not worth while to do anything in this small tub *Dart* way', for if he so says, ten to one he will never do much in a large way. It is the spirit and the feeling that you must be doing something that is the true secret of success. Put pride in your pocket and your shoulder to the wheel and early prejudices under foot, and put that foot down fearlessly, even though it be only on the first rung of the lowliest of ladders; look not back; let your motto be 'Onward ever'. Providence helps those who help themselves. Go ahead and win!

These reflections are quite appropriate to the occasion which they herald—that of my finding myself floating away in the tub *Dart*. Here was I, an M.D. Edinensis, with a long line of Highland ancestors, too numerous to mention, and too dangerous to scrutinise even through their grand baronial walls, turned incipient pig-merchant.

Yes, I floated grandly away up the Tamaki River with the flood-tide, and, stealing up a little creek, we came to where a portage of about half a mile—owing to the interlacing of the waters of the eastern and western harbours—enabled us to reach the head waters of the Manukau.

Walking acrosss the portage we found a canoe, and having transferred to it, my merchandise, *alias* 'trade', we dropped down to the Ngati Whatua *kumara* grounds and fishing station of former acquaintance, at Onehunga, and here we found all the tribe.

'*We*' consisted of the supercargo, and the commander of the *Dart*, who, from his Maori marriage connection, was perfectly conversant with the language of his better-half, so I had him to fall back upon if my own limited knowledge should fail me in the weighty transactions in which I was about to be engaged.

It was immediately given forth that I had come to *hoko* for pigs, as I wanted to stock the island with the unclean animal, and that I also wanted a small supply of potatoes and *kumara* for domestic consumption.

So I spread out my small store of blankets, shirts, printed calico, spades, &c., to tempt the owners of pigs to drive them to a barter market, and I sat me down and began to whistle the tune of *taihoa*, secretly invoking the shade of Job to support me, for I now had it instilled into my youthful impatience that *taihoa* was a power in the land, not to be combated except to one's own great detriment, so I whistled away *'taihoa'* to the English version, 'Hurry no man's cattle', preparing to suffer and be strong to an unlimited extent.

I was not a little startled and surprised, however, that there was not going to be any *taihoa* whatever as to the appropriation of my wares, as a most startling rush was made to *tapu* everything right and left.

This proceeding was performed after the following fashion, the chiefs and chieftainesses being allowed precedence, before the *oi polloi* took up the balance of *tapu*-ing.

When any article was fancied, the intending purchaser took a thrumb from the fringe of his or her mat, and fastened it on to the chosen article. If the selector happened to be wearing a blanket or shirt or mat without a fringe, or wearing *nothing at all,* as was sometimes the case, from which any *tapu*-ing mark could be detached, then a neighbouring flax bush, or piece of flax from a potato kit, supplied the wherewithal to affix the *tapu*.

This once done, no one ever dreamt of disturbing or disputing the choice so made. I saw all my 'trade' rapidly labelled 'sold', by this process, but neither heard nor saw a sign of a grunter being forthcoming.

At last old Kawau came to close quarters, and squatting himself down beside me, he opened fire by propounding the question '*E hia nga tara mo tenei paraikete?*' How many dollars for this blanket? *paraikete* being the nearest approximation the Maori can make to the pronunciation of the word blanket. I repeated the old chief's question with an inquiring stare, as much as to say, ' don't know what you mean', and thought to myself, 'Why the mischief doesn't the old fellow bring me a pig he thinks the value of the blanket?'

'*E hia?*'—How many? repeats the old man.

'*E hia?*' I repeated. 'What have dollars to do with pigs?'

I exclaimed aloud in my own vernacular, quite forgetting he did not understand me.

'*E hia?*' again repeats Kawau, drawling out the word while fumbling with the corner of the blanket he wore, and which at last he succeeded in opening, when out there jerked into his lap quite a small shower of—glittering sovereigns!

Again benignly looking me in the face, and breaking into a smile which caused to curl up still higher the tattooed wave-line at the corners of his mouth, he repeated in the most mellifluous tone—

'*E hia te tara?*'

Why, the old man means what he says after all, but where the devil have all the sovereigns come from?

And on my face wonder must have been so plainly written as I stared at the old man, that he said—

'*Te utu mo te whenua*'. (The payment for the land.)

'Hallo!' I sang out in the most excited manner to the commander of the *Dart*. 'Come here, look here; Kawau has got heaps of sovereigns—payment for land he says.'

'What land?' we both asked in a breath.

'For this land and the Waitemata land', replied Kawau quietly. 'We have been to Kororareka to get the *utu* and sign the *pukapuka,* and this is some of the money.'

'Hurrah! hurrah! hurrah!' shouted I, jumping up. 'The isthmus is bought—the capital fixed—hurrah! hurrah!'

And I there and then extemporized a war-dance, poor old Kawau looking unutterable amazement, and firmly believing I had gone clean mad.

Here was the explanation of the little topsail schooner we had seen from the island slipping in to Orakei bay. The chiefs had been taken up to sign, seal, and deliver the deeds, and get part of their money, and here was some of it glittering before me in veritable proof.

'But Orakei, have you sold that?' I asked.

'*Kahore, kahore!*' (No, no), he said, which word was chorused from a dozen voices all around.

No, indeed! Orakei and its lovely slopes were not sold. The land was higher up the harbour, and cutting across the isthmus to Onehunga, a narrow strip only a little to the west, embracing a large shore frontage to the Waitemata and of very miserable quality. It was a Maori bargain, and he had been equal to the occasion—indeed, when was he not? He always kept the cream of the land, and sold the skimmed milk to the Pakeha. In after years it became proverbial that if in travelling through the country and crossing poor tracts of stunted fern you asked, 'Whose land is this?' the reply would be 'The Queen's land'. 'And these beautiful fertile spots?' 'The land of the Maori, of course; you did not need to ask.'

But enough land, and good land too, had been bought to give a shore on both east and west harbours and transit across the isthmus.

'*E hia nga tara?*' quoth the old man. He was quite shrewd enough to know that, pretty as his gold looked, after all glittering sovereigns were a very useless commodity to him. Wepiha's trading Pakeha had departed; there was not any *whare hoko* from which blankets and tobacco could now be drawn; the gold might remain long enough tied up in the corner of his blanket, and here was a rare chance to get rid of it.

This fact had become patent to the old chief, and he kept constantly repeating his question. But it had also dawned upon me that if I took gold it would be just as useless to me on the island as it was to the old man here, for gold would no more bring forth and multiply in my purse than in the corner of his blanket. But good breeding sows might, if left to themselves, roam over and fatten upon the rich fern-root of Motu-Korea.

'*E hia nga tara?*' persisted Kawau.

'I want pigs', I rejoined.

'*Heaha te pai o te moni?*'—'What is the good of money? I can't put it on my back and wear it, or in my pipe and smoke it. Very good is gold for the Pakeha.'

'And what is the use of gold to me? Sovereigns put on Motu-Korea won't eat up fern-root and multiply—pigs would.'

'*E hoa* (friend of mine) that is what I want my pigs to do for me. I have plenty of fern-root too.'

'But you have lots of pigs, and I have not any at all.'

I thought I had played a good card by that remark.

Silence for some time on the part of Kawau.

'*Kanui pai te koura mo te Pakeha*' ('Exceedingly good is the gold for the white man.')

Not being able to contradict that assertion, I shelved it and played the waiting game. Long silence, the old man deeming he had shut me up. At last I ventured upon saying, 'Exceedingly good is the Pakeha's trade at Motu-Korea—better than gold in the corner of a blanket!'

I thought this remark might serve as a draw.

'*Ae pea*' ('Yes perhaps') at last came from him, his voice assuming a tone of superior wisdom. '*Ae pea* two blankets may become three at Motu-Korea if the rats don't eat them. Rats don't eat gold.'

Well delivered that thrust—a veritable trump card which made me feel the crisis was at hand, and if I could not play a better it looked as if the game was to be the old chief's, and he was going to take the trick.

But a happy idea came to my rescue. 'There is no tribe in the land, then, but the Ngati Whatua, and no pigs in the land but your pigs.'

And I rose and began deliberately to unfasten his *tapu* mark from the articles he had chosen. This *was* the ace of trumps.

'*Haere mai nei, haere mai nei* (Come here, come here, and sit down)', said the old man quickly, 'and let us *korero*.'

He could not stand seeing his *tapu* marks removed, which meant that I was going away with all my small wares.

And so we sat down, and it thus came about that I had to bring my shrewdest wits to bear upon this my maiden

H

transaction in the commercial world, and I only just managed to prove equal to the great small occasion.

After much *korero*-ing and long battling we arranged a compromise over the glittering gold so much despised.

But I only made it a drawn game—half in gold, half in produce—half gold old Kawau's winning card and half produce mine.

And so I departed in peace—thirty gold sovereigns in hand, sixty pigs driven on foot.

Ho for Motu-Korea!

CHAPTER VII

The Capital is Born to Us : The Flagstaff that never was Erected

THE solitude of the little island of Motu-Korea hath departed—yes, for evermore departed.

No longer solitary are the waters of the Waitemata, stretching away from our primitive *whare* on the beach to the foot of the western ranges—never to be solitary again in our day nor for many generations yet to follow. How many who shall say?

There lies at anchor, a little way above Orakei Bay, a three-masted vessel.

Boats are plying to and from the ship and shore. White tents are seen dotting the fern-slopes, reclaiming them from the wilderness, and making the hitherto solitary place glad.

Only a single ship, a few tents, and a handful of the Saxon race.

They have planted their feet on a far-distant land, and in a little time to what a great end this small beginning shall grow!

The pilgrim fathers have pitched their tents on that shore, a spot in the unreclaimed wilderness has been named a name, an embryo capital has been born, the flag of England floats over it, and under its protecting folds a new people will arise and a future nation create a history.

And as we looked away along the waters from our place of Motu-Korea we saw our long-hoped-for infant born to us, and solitude fled for evermore.

Our little island is no longer a place unknown to and unseen of men, for daily, unnumbered generations of the dwellers on the heights of the Remuera slopes, when they look to the east as they rise to their day of toil, shall see lying between them and the rising sun the crater summit of Motu-Korea illumined by the morning rays.

How quickly it had come upon us, and yet how long a few weeks of our solitary sojourn had appeared on the island!

Day after day we never saw a sign of life as we gazed all around, looking into every distant bay, watching the headlands, and wearying to see a sail round some promontory and gladden the eye, but in vain. Beautiful Nature enchanted the sight, but gave that feeling of utter solitude that creates unrest. What though it might be said that 'All save the face of man was divine' in the landscape? The want of that undivine thing was just what we had felt so severely, and when that missing feature arrived we felt once again that we belonged to the outer world, and that the time was at last at hand when we must take our place in it and form a part of it.

We were not doomed to wait long before we came in contact with our fellow-men, but the occasion was not of that happy and agreeable kind which our rising hopes had pictured. In fact, our first experience was of anything but a satisfactory nature. The first wave of civilization which reached our hitherto benighted shore was of a decidedly cooling character, being none other than an attempt to dispossess us of our little island home.

I had just returned from Waiomu. I had been there to ask Kanini to come to the island to receive the payment for it—he had as yet only got the earnest-money—and he had brought me back in his largest war-canoe, and it thus happened he was on the island when what I am about to narrate occurred.

It was only a day or two after the pitching of the Government officials' tents which now marked the spot of the future capital that we saw a canoe making for the island, and steering directly for our *whare*. It seemed to make but very little way considering the very vigorous manner in which the paddlers worked. As the canoe neared the shore we soon discovered the reason—a large spar was being towed astern. We also saw two Pakehas were in the canoe, and that my old friend Kawau—old '*E hia nga tara*'—was in the place of dignity and was steersman.

When the canoe reached the beach the two Pakehas landed, not only themselves, but also some picks and shovels. To our inquiry for what purpose they had come, and for what possible purpose the picks and shovels could be, we were informed that the Deputy-Governor—here indeed we were at once face to face with civilization—yes, the Deputy-Governor was following in their wake; meanwhile they were to go to the top of the hill, and there dig a deep hole, into which the spar they had brought, and which the natives were going to drag up, was to be put; from it was then to float the British ensign, as the Deputy-Governor was going to take possession of the island in the name of Her Majesty the Queen!

Such was the interesting ceremony about to be performed to inaugurate our first contact with the 'civilized faculty' which had arrived to replace the savage one, leading us to believe that we had better have remained under the latter.

Whilst we were extracting this highly-interesting information, Kawau, on landing and seeing Kanini squatting on the shore, of course made a bee-line with his nose, for that of Kanini, and they were duly rubbed in the lugubrious *tangi* of welcome; after which the *korero* began. Of course it was pipes and tobacco first, and of course *taihoa* the dragging up the spar.

And *taihoa* the dragging the spar remained. Even after the Deputy-Governor's boat came in sight not a move was made—the spar lay where the ebbing tide had left it on the beach.

The state of the case was this:—Kanini had told Kawau

how he had sold the island to *his* two Rangatira Pakehas, and he would like to see the Governor that would take it away from them—put up a flag-staff indeed!—would they?—where would he be, and his tribe?

Kawau drew the required inference, and said the spar might lie on the beach to the crack of doom—of course Maori intellect had invented equally expressive words, and had them in their phraseology—yes, might lie there for ever as far as his dragging it up the hill was concerned.

So when the Deputy-Governor arrived he found his emissary Kawau squatted, pipe in mouth, alongside of Kanini, and he was at once greeted with *'Taihoa te rakau!'* (By-and-by the spar!).

I was now more convinced than ever that *'taihoa' was* the most wonderful and powerful word that had ever been invented—an unequalled talisman.

'Taihoa te rakau!' sang out Kawau before even the boat could touch the beach, for he knew that the moment the Deputy-Governor put foot on shore the question would be asked, 'Why have you not dragged up the spar?' But *'taihoa te rakau'* was sufficient warning that something was up, and that, *taihoa,* the explanation would be given.

We welcomed the Deputy-Governor as he stepped on shore, his mission notwithstanding, and at a glance we saw he was every inch a gentleman, and we flattered ourselves we were not even the sixteenth part of an inch short of being the same ourselves!

We soon fraternised. He told us 'he had a disagreeable duty to perform—in fact, he really felt very much embarrassed—had not the slightest idea of the pleasure which awaited him in coming here. His Excellency the Governor must have been quite misinformed. It was said a pair of Pakeha-Maori sawyers had taken possession of the island, and, in fact, he had been instructed to summarily bundle them off neck and crop, and to take possession of the island, as it was required for Government purposes.'

Of course we had our little story to tell, that there sat Kanini, chief of the Ngati Tamatera, and we were under *his* protecting wing, Her Majesty the Queen notwithstanding, and that we had not the slightest intention of foregoing our title to our little island.

The Deputy accepted the situation, and said he must so far obey his instructions as to take nominal possession, meanwhile would we join him in having some luncheon?

We heartily thanked him, accepting his invitation, and candidly telling him that had he not brought his own it could only have been the hospitality of pork and potatoes that we could have offered, for as yet we were destitute of any more civilized supplies.

The fact was, the 'taking possession' had been converted into a nice little picnic excursion, the captain of the vessel in which the staff of officials had come having brought the Deputy in his boat along with a brace of officials, so we reaped the benefit in partaking of such a repast as we had not revelled in since the long-past time of the Herekino *table d'hôte* days.

Whilst we were busy chatting over and eating our luncheon, one of the boat's crew had been told to quietly splice the ensign to the end of an oar and stick it into the soft sand of the beach. The ceremony was thus unceremoniously performed, hardly anyone noticing it, and the Deputy obeyed the red-tape instructions about taking possession.

It was well that the old Kanini did not understand or notice this ceremony, or most assuredly Her Majesty's ensign, instead of floating thus modestly at the end of an oar, would have ignominiously 'bit the dust', only on this occasion it would have been a clean gravelly beach!

The visit had its pleasant side, too, for we learned with extreme satisfaction that the site of the future capital had really been fixed upon, three bays higher up the harbour than Orakei, that the surveyors would soon be at work laying off the town lots for the first sale, which was expected to come off in about three months, that the

Government had brought down a gang of workmen—sawyers, carpenters, blacksmiths, etc.—to proceed with the erection of the required Government buildings, and that Kawau and his tribe had been pressed into service—nothing loath—to erect meanwhile *whares* for the head officials.

And the Deputy-Governor took his departure, proffering to us his best services when we 'removed to town'. How civilized it sounded, to be sure! and when we saw him pull away, the principal impression left upon us was, that we had spent an uncommonly pleasant afternoon, accompanied with an all-overish feeling of having partaken of an uncommonly good luncheon.

. But there remained relics of that visit of the Deputy-Governor's which it took many years to efface.

The hole *was* dug more than six feet in the very highest point of the crater summit, into which the spar was *never* put, and long it took before the sides crumbled in and filled it up.

And the spar lay washed up at high-water mark, now and again at spring tides shifting a little its position along the beach; but there it lay until its sap rotted away, and then it yielded snatches of firewood to encamping Maoris in long-after days when they touched at the island when bringing provisions to the capital's early settlers and first citizens.

Never more was the little island a place lying in the mid-channel of waters which showed no signs of life, for now the *raupo* sail of the Maori canoe was rarely wanting, soon to be replaced by the calico sail, which, with white wings, dotted the surrounding waters and marked still more brightly that the expanse of the inlet leading from Te Hauraki to Waitemata *had* now become a great thoroughfare to the new home of the Pakeha.

And when the sun rose it lighted up with its morning rays not only the crater summit of Motu-Korea, but the white tents of the embryo capital on Waitemata's sloping shores.

CHAPTER VIII

We Change the Current of our Lives : We Visit our Newly-born Child

THE Deputy-Governor's visit had, no doubt, left us with a small skeleton in the corner of our *raupo whare,* but we stowed it away out of sight, and it got lost for the time being, though afterwards it was brought to light and aired again, and by no less a person than His Excellency the Governor *in propriâ personâ,* but his visit to the island I shall hereafter chronicle.

The Deputy's visit had meanwhile left a most pleasing impression behind, for we not only felt we were once again within the pale of civilization, such as it was, but the prospect which had led us to come to live on the island was an accomplished fact.

Our anticipations, when standing on the crater summit of Remuera, that on the shore of the isthmus somewhere or other the future capital would arise, were now fulfilled, and the object for which we had purchased the island—a resting-place until we could settle at the newborn capital itself—was gained.

The first chapter of our new life was, we felt, now nearly closed. The island as a pig-station was all very well when we were compelled to consider ourselves the solitary Pakeha guardians of the whole broad waters of the Waitemata, but now that the infant capital was born to us we were anxious to adopt our child at once and go and live with it.

H2

So we were now about to enter on the second chapter of our lives in Maoridom—one which would have but small connection with the past. The past was a past associated with Maoris and Pakeha-Maoris, with Wepihas, Pamas, the good old Kanini, and with Kawau, native scenes, customs, and Maori life; but now we felt we were entering on the first steps of civilization. True, we saw, and could well foreshadow, that the path would be a wearily rough one for many a long day to come. But we had arrived at the new starting-point of our lives, so we now took counsel together what course we ought to pursue.

Until now we had only had one fixed determination, and that was to become purchasers of town lots in the new capital and settle down there, acting as very small landsharks with the very small capital we had to invest, and with some rather hazy sort of idea that we would practise our respective professions.

But when we came to analyse this crude idea, and reduce it to its component prospects, so to speak, we could not flatter ourselves that there would be a very wide field in which to exercise the undoubted talents we both believed we respectively possessed! We quite came to the conclusion that we should be wasting the fragrance of sound law and good physic on the desert air of a yet-to-be-populated capital, and that there would not be a legitimate field for our great, though still very youthful, energies, mentally and bodily, in mere quill-driving and pill-making.

On its being mooted whether we should turn merchants, I had no hesitation in declaring, with that fine self-assumption which pertains to very young manhood's years, that, as far as I was concerned, *I* would 'throw physic to the dogs' if he would 'cut the law', and we would start as merchants, commission-agents, pig and potato brokers, anything and everything, in both a large and a small way!

What though *my* experience was *nil,* or, say, confined

to and summed up in that great '*E hia nga tara*' transaction on the shore of Onehunga, what though I was
only green from my university and taking my medical
degrees, and did not even know what a promissory note
was, far less had discounted one, and as for the term
'*del credere*', it might as well have been Hebrew or any
other to me unknown language; what though, in a general way, I was all round just as ignorant of commerce
as any village school-boy?

After all, the field of commerce in the young capital
must be of a very restricted kind for some years to come;
we could surely, in learning our lessons, keep pace with
its growth, and get on quite nicely. And what an inspiring idea it was that we should be instrumental in 'developing the resources of our adopted country', and be the
fathers of the commerce of a future nation! Was that to
count for nothing? Most assuredly not, and we worked
up that idea until it stood foremost as the grand beacon-
light by which we were to steer.

Yes, quite unknown to ourselves, we kept jingling up
this fine patriotic idea with the two or three sixpences
in our pockets, until we quite believed it constituted a
prominent element in the decision we had come to as
to the new path in life, which we expected to convert all
our sixpences into bright gold pieces!

At the same time, of course, we should be doing
wonders in developing the resources of our adopted
country!

The future course of our lives was all fixed and determined upon, with the happy self-conceit of youth, one
forenoon as we jauntily paced up and down the shingly
beach, looking now and again away towards the white
tents of the infant capital, and looking away into the
future, conjuring up a mighty city, and ourselves very
big men indeed in it.

Meanwhile our existence was not altogether of a
character to prepare us for this great future—potato and
pumpkin growing, and having a turn through the fern

to see how pigs improved the occasion, were not employments to sharpen the intellectual faculties. The dire necessity of getting through certain given daily domestic avocations pretty well consumed the day. These had to be done, however disagreeable the doing them; we were our own cooks, our own maids-of-all-work, our own laundresses. I much fear the proximity of a native village might have made one or the other of us succumb to the temptation to marry a chieftainess to escape from these domestic drudgeries—in fact, one night, just to see which way the wind blew, I propounded the question, and proposed drawing lots to see which was to be the victim, but the thing was not recognised even as a joke! We did make the best attempt we could to prevent our brains from getting cobwebbed over and mouldy by devoting our evenings to such literary pursuits as half-a-dozen books afforded. The pages of our Shakespeare were illumined dimly enough certainly, and by nothing half so civilized as even a farthing rushlight. A piece of rag on a stick planted into a pannikin of fat was anything but sightly to look upon, and not a little disagreeable to the olfactories, but it did brighten up the darkness of our evenings when combined with the light of the great poet; better this than go to bed at sunset, which would have been the only alternative.

After the passing away of three weeks since the Deputy-Governor's visit we could no longer refrain from paying town a visit. We had noticed the white tents and *raupo* houses becoming more freely dotted over the slopes of the bay which looked towards our island, so we thought we would go to have a look at our adopted child, and see how it was getting on in the swaddling-clothes in which we saw it becoming clothed.

So one fine calm morning, locking up our *whare* door by tying it with a piece of flax, and leaving Tartar in charge we got into our canoe and paddled up to town.

As we skirted Orakei Bay we saw no change there save an extra number of canoes on the beach; it was now even as we had first seen it half a year ago, when on its shore we had eaten our famous pigeon-soup and did *not* succeed in purchasing the Remuera slopes.

The next two little bays lay sleeping as of old in Nature's primitive state, but in the bays higher up the harbour primitive Nature reigned no longer; she had been put to flight for long generations in the future, if not for evermore.

The last time we had pulled past that shore the wild curlew stalked the beach and took to wing—it stalked the beach no longer, and had been forever put to flight.

Sawyers' huts were on the shore; logs of timber strewed the beach.

It was the wilderness no longer; civilized man had now planted his foot upon the strand and set his mark upon the shore, and was now wresting the wilderness from Nature's unreclaimed dominion, and that spot had now a name, and was known by the unromantic but practical one of Mechanics' Bay. And then we came to the pretty slopes of the little bay, where the white tents, which we could see so plainly from the island, nestled amongst the brushwood, and this spot had a name also equally unromantic, but appropriate—Official Bay, for here the first magnates of the land had squatted themselves down; and then we rounded a point and glided into the Commercial Bay of the capital.

The capital!—a few boats and canoes on the beach, a few tents and break-wind huts along the margin of the bay, and then—a sea of fern stretching away as far as the eye could reach.

Small indeed was the change: still, did it not tell us that here our infant capital was now born to us—was struggling into existence in the first swaddling-clothes of its first month's infancy?

Had we not waited in our solitary home on our little island with an abiding faith that this very infant capital would be born to us on these very shores? And we now saw it an existent fact, and we were greatly content and accepted the parentage, and there and then consecrated our coming years to fostering it with care.

Ah! beautiful then, my dear children, was the wild spot in its still unreclaimed native beauty which had just been christened the capital of Poenamo; ever beautiful, whether as then unadorned save by Nature's hand, or as now, adorned in the vestments in which she is now robed and which become her so well, as upon her lovely shores she sits the Queen of Beauty, unrivalled in the Great South Land.

We appropriately made our advent to the *not* stirring quay of the capital in our modest canoe, dug at the forest of Waiomu. What a sensation we should excite now could we only arrive as we then arrived, with blue flannel shirts serving as overcoats, paddle in hand, and the *kauri* log fashioned as a little boat, and many flax leaves knotted together our only painter?

But we created no surprise then; no group of curious idlers collected to see us step out of our little canoe; no one saw us but ourselves, and we hauled it up on the beach high and dry, and betook ourselves straight away through a fern footpath to the *whare* of the Deputy-Governor, who had perched himself on a cliff point which commanded a view of the whole harbour.

And kindly he greeted us; and we asked him how the young capital prospered and how its survey proceeded, and what prospect there was of a first sale of town lots taking place.

And the Deputy-Governor, waving his hand from his cliff point of view, and stretching it towards Official Bay, said—'You see what is going on there; our Maori neighbours have come to the rescue, and are busily at work building *whares* for us'. And then turning round he again waved his hand away towards Mechanics' Bay, and said—'And there you can see the Government sawyers hard at work, and in due course of time we shall have some offices erected, and a roof over our heads, under which the surveyors will be able to map out their work; but, to tell you the truth, we have been more busy housing ourselves than doing anything else, and I am afraid I cannot say that the survey has even yet been begun, and the summer will certainly be well over before it can be finished, and there is no possibility of there being any sale of town land for some months to come.

'And as to that little affair of my instructions to bundle a certain pair of supposed Pakeha-Maori sawyers off Motu-Korea, his Excellency has not vouchsafed to take any notice of the report I sent him on the subject, or transmit any further turning off instructions—not likely he would after what I wrote him.'

And so we betook ourselves back to our canoe, and we saw the little tents and *whares* basking calmly and peacefully in the warm sun, and we got a glimpse of a stray figure flitting through high fern; but the only noise in this embryo capital that fell upon the ear was the low chant of the Maori worker, as he leisurely, on purest *taihoa* principles, tied the *raupo* on to the walls of a *whare* he was building for the Pakeha—the Pakeha who would overrun the fair land on which he had now first set his foot.

The infant capital was still asleep in its first nursery cradle, and it was evident that we might safely leave it to slumber yet awhile before we took it by the hand.

And so we two pioneer fathers who had sojourned at Motu-Korea in anticipation of the great event which we had now seen realised did not 'shake the dust off our feet as we departed that city' because it was of our adoption, and already our hearts warmed towards it, and as we took our seats in our little canoe we raised our paddles high in the air, and plunging them into the waters of the Waitemata we sent a shower of spray as a christening blessing on that shore to which we hoped, ere long, to return and claim as our future home.

CHAPTER IX

How we Shave a Pig

WE paddled back to our meanwhile island home, carrying away with us the impression that the capital certainly still wore but a very infantile face, but, nevertheless, that it was fair to look upon, and we had a feeling of pleased contentment that with its growth it would still grow in beauty, and that its advancing years would never belie the fair promise of its youth, nor did they ever.

As we neared the island we received a most vociferous welcome from Tartar, who dashed into the water to receive us—a famous water-dog he was amongst many other wonderful qualities. Of course we found the flax lock of our *whare* even as we had left it, for we were still in advance of that civilization which was to give us Pakeha thieves; but hereafter I shall have to narrate to you how we became victims to that species of civilization, and, strange to say, Motu-Korea was the scene of the first great exploit of the kind.

The last month of spring had now arrived, and we found ourselves passing through a climate unrivalled in its beauty, and which gave a physical enjoyment of life that seemed to make the mere fact of living an ecstatic happiness.

Our importation of pig stock had obliged us to fence in our small garden, which we did with a dry scoria wall, and we worked away at small improvements, as it was our intention when we removed to town to try and get some one to come and take charge of our large and rapidly-increasing families of pigs, in order that the most should be made of our pig-run speculation, and that the fruits of our labours should not be thrown away when the capital created a market.

Meanwhile, until we should become absorbed as citizens in that capital, we had to eat and drink, and the stock of corned pork we laid in from Wepiha became exhausted.

We tacitly put off the evil day of taking the required steps to refill our 'harness cask', but the unpleasant duty was at last forced upon us, as digging *pipi* out of the beach at low water had become quite intolerable, and, latterly, *pipi* had been the only addition to our potato fare.

It looked as if the nearer we got towards the 'capital' point of civilization the farther away we got from it in a social and domestic way!

At Waiomu, amongst our tattooed savage friends, we had all menial work taken off our hands; but now, with the young capital staring us in the face, we had to be our own everything. We had hitherto, with an equanimity worthy of all praise—at least, we most decidedly thought so—submitted to the performance of every kind of domestic work, but the climax had arrived now that it was a case of acting the butcher!

There was no help for it, however; it was either kill a pig or continue to go without meat, and we had now gone so long without it that we were beginning to realize the reason why Maoris eat each other now and again, just to vary the monotony of their fish and vegetable diet.

So one morning saw us pushing through the high fern, with Tartar at our heels, to try and spot one of the fattest of those sixty porkers which had given me my first commercial lesson. The rich free soil of the island made the fern-root easily grubbed up, so that a hog, if full-grown, soon became fat and kept so without any other food, and made pork of great delicacy, perfectly different to the same article at home.

After some little hunting about we succeeded in singling out the intended victim, and, pointing it out to Tartar, he soon had it by the ear, and held it until we came up and tied a flax string to the foot, when we drove it home to the place of execution.

Here we had prepared a nice bed of fern on which our victim was to be scraped—we had kindled fires under our largest pots for the boiling water—the scalding-tub was at hand, and all was ready.

There lay the knife, long and sharp, but who was to use that knife had never been alluded to by either of us. Each hugged to his soul the belief it would be the other, and not himself.

We threw the pig on its side amid much loud music given forth not only by the pig but Tartar, who added to the deafening row. I got my knees on the animal's head to keep him down, and thought I had played a fine card.

'There is the knife. Now is your time', said I.

'For me!—I stick a pig! How do I know where its heart is? Come, go ahead—it is all in the way of your profession; don't be chicken-hearted.'

Whereat I looked at the ugly long sharp knife, and roared, to be heard above the awful squealing:

'Can't do it!'

'Nothing for dinner!'

'Dinner be damned!'

'Only one dig, and all's over.'

'Dig yourself.'

'Then we must dig *pipi! pipi! pipi!*' each '*pipi*' yelled out louder and louder.

Then came a furious struggle from poor porker. We both jumped up—porker staggered away.

Somehow I had given him his quietus.

'Ugh! beastly!' came from me as I chucked away the knife.

'Bravo! You really did it splendidly—positively quite a scientific thrust. The poor brute is dead already—believe you have gone straight to the heart. Don't look so woe-begone; it's all over now.'

Yes, the sticking was, but something awaited us which proved a much worse job than killing the beast—the scraping it.

We lifted up our victim and soused it well in the boiling water in the scalding-tub, turning it over and walloping it about in a wonderful manner, so that every bit of the carcass should get a good dip in the boiling water, and then lifting it out we placed it on the bed of fern, expecting to see the hair come peeling off.

But, lo! great was our disappointment, for hardly a hair, let alone a bristle, came away; it all stuck most pertinaciously to the brute, defying all our efforts to remove it.

'The water certainly was boiling', I remarked.

'I thought so too, but let us pour some more over the brute; we have a spare supply in that other boiler.'

And more we did pour, but not a bit would the hair come off.

Pleasant work it was, to be sure, with a strong hot sun overhead, the lifting the carcass into the tub again, then out again, in the vain attempt to properly scald it and get the hair off.

Ah, poor greenhorns! you may scrape and scrape, but the hair off that pig you will never scrape. By one process only can you now get that hair off, and that is—by shaving!

The water ought *not* to have been boiling. A bucketful of cold water should have been dashed in to take it off the boiling-point, and then had porker been submerged the hair would have all come away. We had what is termed *set* it, and thoroughly well set it was, and no mistake. But this was an experience which came to us too late, and that pig we had to shave, and a nice little job it was. The porker did not look at all sightly when we hung it up on the branch of a tree; it was not that beautiful white carcass that delighteth the eye of a butcher as he hangs it, lemon in mouth, in his stall. Alas! our poor

porker looked as if it was rejoicing in a beard of a week's
growth.

But this was our first and our last experience in pig-
sticking—we never required to kill another. The event-
uality was one I had not anticipated when learning up
experiences in my 'ain kintrie' by practical lessons for the
future of an emigrant's life. I had, in anticipation of being
thrown on my own resources as a sheep-squatter in Australia, taken a lesson before leaving home of how to kill
a sheep and deal with the carcass, but I little thought then
that pigs in Maoriland were to be my fate. The knowledge
I had gained in the sheep line, however, stood me in good
stead, and but for it we might have made a far greater
mess before we reached the stage of hanging up the opened
carcass of our shaved pig.

There is romance and reality in the early settler's life.
The romance is ever prominently narrated, and travels
far and wide and deludes many a victim, but the stern
realities ever remain an unknown quantity, except to those
who have to pass through the ordeal, and the remembrances are often painful enough.

'Tis well the future of our lives is a sealed book, or we
should never have nerve to face in cold blood what comes
to us in life as the 'inevitable', and which we go through
because we must and can't help it.

Had I known I should have to play the butcher in
killing and scalding pigs ten to one I should have turned
up an aristocratic nose at the very idea, and seen emigration further. Perhaps I was none the worse for having
killed that pig, but *certes* I was none the better; and had
I gone on having such work to do, *certes* some shade of
refinement must have gone to the wall, but that one pig-
sticking was the alpha and omega of that work, and right
glad was I. Of rough hard work we had any amount
before us, but we took to it pleasantly and with a will as
part of the inevitable that was our portion.

But none the less did we rejoice that pig-sticking and
shaving of the kind we had encountered was for ever a
thing of the past.

CHAPTER X

We Adopt our Child

THE first month of summer was now drawing to a close. Christmas—not white snow-clad Christmas as at home, but the bright and brilliant floral Christmas of the sunny Great South Land, was at hand.

My last Christmas, and first one away from the parental roof, had been spent where the 'experienced surgeon' got eclipsed by the 'cow', and where I walked on shore to try my fortune with the world.

The year which had elapsed had brought its experiences, and a certain amount of my utter greenness had given way to a modicum of that worldly wisdom without which no man can elbow his way beyond the ordinary bread and butter of life.

Now I had the ambition to soar higher than this, and nothing less than cakes and ale *ad libitum* was going to satisfy my youthful aspirations.

The inexperienced youth of a surgeon had now thrown physic to the dogs, and was with a still greater inexperience, and with a cool self-reliance belonging only to the self-conceit of immature years, going to boldly try his unfledged wings in the flight of commerce.

I once laboured under the delusion that modesty was the one beautiful trait in my character, but when I revise my past life I am a little shaken in that belief, and now have more than a mere suspicion that there was what other people would designate as egregious conceit stamped on one or two passages of the early career of my young manhood, or else how could I have had the presumption to take the appointment of the 'experienced surgeon'? And now I had dubbed myself merchant without ever having 'walked the hospitals' of commerce.

Truly the boldness of ignorance is often bliss. Happy indeed that we are not always wise before our wisdom teeth are cut—Heaven is my witness I was not—but as I never fell into any great mishaps I suppose a kind Providence must have taken compassion on me and bridged over the difficulties.

The time had at last arrived when I must make my new departure in life and commence the *rôle* of merchant. The die was cast, for better for worse I had taken the leap, and must risk whether I landed on my feet or came ignominiously to the ground.

The tub *Dart* lay once again at anchor a few cables' length from the shore, opposite our *whare,* and we were plying the canoe to and fro. I was taking my departure for the capital to establish its first mercantile firm! There in the hold of the schooner lay the now historical little tent. You have seen it put to many various uses at various places, but the climax of its history had now come; it was about to be pitched at the embryo capital to represent the business premises of the embryo firm, and therein I was to be representative thereof. The senior partner could not be spared as yet from the graver stake we had in our pig-run, and as it had to be watched over by the more experienced member of the firm, he had to remain on the island for a time, looking forward to joining me when I had succeeded in getting a Maori *whare* erected to replace the tent as more befitting business premises.

By the time this was accomplished we hoped either to have sold off all our pigs or got hold of some one to live on the island and look after the rapidly-increasing litters. Of course the presence of the senior partner was indispensable at the founding of the firm, so 'we twa' sailed away in great state in the tub *Dart,* the Waiomu towing astern, and we dropped anchor off the capital. And the senior and junior paddled to shore in the Waiomu, not only themselves but the firm's premises and all the stock-in-trade with which it was thought necessary to commence business.

The inventory of effects had not been an arduous task; for the senior, wise in his generation, and in the knowledge of the supreme greenness of his junior partner, had deemed that all that was necessary for him in the establishing the name of the firm was a couple of three-legged pots, a quart tin pot, and a pannikin, which, by a figure of speech, might be said to represent the hardware department; the soft goods department was as yet only represented by the contents of the junior's personal effects in his sea-chest; and as to the provision department—well, there *was* a little tea and sugar to the good, with some kits of potatoes and a few junks of corned pork. The stock-in-trade of a general merchant in the days which I depict in a newly-formed settlement was of the character graphically summed up in the old phrase 'from a needle to an anchor'.

So we reared aloft the poles of our tent, stretched the canvas over the roof-tree, and then—we shook each other cordially by the hand, and thus standing under it wished each other joy, and declared the firm was now born to the capital and an existent fact!

The business transacted that summer evening by the two partners was a large speculation in the line of bedding fern—as much as could be stored on the premises, and then the partners, resting from their labours, might have been seen sitting on the ground, a wreath of blue smoke from the fire in front of them curling overhead.

The sun set to the music of a pot of water hubble-bubbling, the stars shone out and became brightly brilliant by the time the quart pot of water was boiling to make the tea, and just as the moon rose the partners retired within the folding canvas of their tent-premises to practically prove if their 'fern bedding' venture was of that genuine quality which would insure their peaceful slumbers.

And thus it was that that first firm of the capital of Poenamo started, and that firm has endured even unto the present day, through two score years! And the then verdiest of verdi juniors has now got all his innocent greenness taken out of him; many was the eye-opener he got, but he has survived not only to become senior but sole partner, and lives to tell all this to his children.

But I am not going to travel over all these long years with a narrative of what would prove but a dreary personal record of the everyday routine of life. But before the capital reached the stage when one day became a repetition of another, it passed through epochs peculiarly its own, and although I have already written more than enough for my first half of my manuscript, I shall still write on a few pages to bring these epochs to a close. I shall then have to cease the chronicling of what have hitherto been almost purely personal memoirs, and my narrative will assume the character of the 'Early History of the Colony'.

CHAPTER XI

The Capital of Poenamo in 1841 : How we Lived then

TO travel away forty years back in one's past life and portray scenes then occurring would not be an easy task unless those scenes had a character peculiarly their own, and stood out in bold relief and marked contrast to the ordinary everyday routine of life.

Forty years ago it is now, and yet how vividly does the dawning year of 1841 and the primitive capital with its handful of people rise before me!

Ah! how many have passed away, and how few remain to me now with whom I acted as the pilgrim fathers of those days! Few indeed are we now; on the fingers of one hand almost can I number them. We are even as so many moss-o'ergrown milestones, ancient relics which marked the road for a past generation which has already travelled to the journey's end.

Yes! the wintry snow of age has blanched our heads, proclaiming the many years which lie buried in the past, and that our course has nearly run.

Yet how vividly rises before me the picture as I used to look upon it when, rising from my fern bed, I folded back my tent-door, and smelt the sweet fresh dew-scent in the air, and saw the rippling tide-wave wash the beach!

How calm and dreamy and peaceful was the primitive life, waiting in expectancy—all waiting in hopeful expectancy—such a bright future conjured up.

We were all squatting, each in the little spot which fancy had dictated, and the day of rivalry was still in the future; there was no envying of a neighbour's superiority or greater fortune; we were all steeped in a passive equality, all hail fellow well met; we were as one family, with a distinction—and that distinction was only the Red Tape one! But we all smiled benignly on the little airs Red Tape put on in the attempt to enshrine itself in a very milk-and-water exclusiveness; for from the top-sawyer of Red Tape down to the veritable top-sawyer and his mate below in the Government sawpits we all gave each other *le beau jour,* and had a passing word of kindness to say when we met among the high fern footpaths or at the landing-place at the beach.

It would have been useless for Red Tape to stand on its dignity; we all elbowed each other so intimately and were so isolated that familiarity ceased to breed contempt and happily engendered the feeling of that good-fellowship which arises where any small band of men are thrown together far away from their other fellow-men and their fatherland.

We had our little jokes, and would ask how Red Tape was this morning in *Exclusion* Bay, for Red Tape had tabooed for itself an Official Bay, known to this day by that name, and did not allow any squatting in it, unless by first obtaining the Surveyor-General's consent. This grand-titled functionary had been passed on to us from our nearest sister colony, and was next in importance to our Deputy-Governor, so we christened Official Bay *Exclusion* Bay, and it held that name long after the first sale of town lots killed for ever the exclusive monopoly.

Then as Commercial Bay was a horribly long name, altogether too high-sounding (except on the Surveyor-General's map) for the pig and potato bartering with the Maoris which took place there, and as the only building erected on it of wood which the capital could boast was a small Government store, the bay at once became Store Bay. Where the sawyers were at work retained its legitimate name of Mechanics' Bay; but there was still another bay where sawyers also were at work, and which immediately became known as Waipiro Bay*, the Maori word for spirits, *alias* stinking water, for much rum was consumed there.

I have now given you the distinctive names of the localities of the young capital, which was now making quite a grand show with its increasing tents and huts dotted over these four bays. But it was a handful of houses and a handful of people only, all peeping out at each other from amongst the scrub and six-feet-high fern all around.

My large establishment, representing not only the firm's business premises but the resident partner's place of abode, consisted, as of old, of the historical tent. It had been pitched where a little trickling thread of water ran past, and I had dug a little well which gave me a plentiful supply, and got hold of an old flour-barrel to put in the hole.

I had also fenced myself off from the gaze of passengers, as the great thoroughfare from Store to Exclusion Bay passed in front of my tent. I had stuck up some poles and clothed them with *ti*-tree, so that I might have a screen behind which I could carry on all my domestic duties. Don't think I was ashamed to be seen performing these—not a bit of it; I never was, and I look back with pride and pleasure to all I had to go through in those days; it was only that innate modesty of mine which rebelled against being a prominent figure on the scene! I used to get up at sunrise, often before it, and go away foraging for wood, which I brought home from a not far-distant patch of brushwood. When the town became more populous this became exhausted, and then the Waiomu took us to the opposite shore of the harbour, and we brought over a plentiful supply.

At the back of my fence I had rigged up a triangle, from which hung a hook on which to suspend my gipsy

[* Afterwards known as Freeman's Bay.]

pot, and the fireplace was backed round with large blocks of scoria stone to prevent my fence from being burnt down. Here I did my modest cooking to the old oft-told *menu,* pork and potatoes—not a sheep or herd of oxen had yet reached the capital, neither butcher nor baker had yet appeared on the field. We all were still our own cooks and hewers of wood and drawers of water, and jolly and well and happy every one of us looked. If there *was* any slightly careworn trace on anyone's face, it was only on the Surveyor-General's for he had survey on the brain and didn't need to cook *his* own dinner; if he only had, he would have been as jolly as the rest of us.

But sometimes my cooking came to grief; it was not always fair-weather work in this direction, for sometimes such foul weather came that I was *hors de combat,* and all *hors-d'œuvres* became a delusion and a by-word instead of a by-dish.

This would happen when one of the north-easters set in, not only blowing great guns, but raining cats and dogs, when my firewood got soaked, and making a fire outside was impossible.

Then came the tug of war for dinner, and how the dinner came, and what it was, I suppose you would hardly believe unless convinced by the faithful extract from a journal I kept in those days, in which, in half-a-dozen words, I summed up each evening what had happened since the morning.

Now here is an extract bearing date *Friday, first day of January, 1841*:

'The happy New Year came, blowing great guns from the north-east—raining like cats and dogs—postponed breakfast to see if the day would clear up—tried to boil some potatoes for dinner—could not succeed for the rain —commissariat at zero, no cold meat left—had to dine off some of yesterday's cold potatoes—and a drink of water! In the evening half-nipped my eyes out of my head with smoke trying to boil a pannikin of water inside the tent —only half succeeded—had a miserable cup of tea.'

Now what do you think of that for a jolly New Year's Day? I wonder whether the entry ought to be put to the credit side of 'romance' or debtor side of 'reality' of early settling? Very primitive were our ways, as I have already stated. We had parsons without churches and magistrates without courts, but we scrambled through our divinity and our law somehow or other, so that we should be held in esteem as a Christian and properly-behaved people.

For instance, here is an entry of date 15th May: 'To-day saw Mr. —— sitting in front of his *whare* administering justice under the canopy of heaven.'

And of the necessity of this open-air-court administration of justice I had a convincing proof, for here is what is entered: '31st.—On returning in the evening to my tent, found a drunken man comfortably snoring away on my bed!' I suppose I would rather he had been up before the administrator of justice under the canopy of heaven that morning, when perhaps he would have been cared for and not have invaded my tent. As for lying down on my bed, I could forgive him for that, for having stumbled into the tent he saw an empty crockery-crate, and he bundled himself down on the top of it. He could not know *that* was my bedstead to keep me from the damp ground, but at this date it had become rainy, and I had already grown luxurious and began to have more exalted ideas than the fern bed on the tent floor!

But though we had the inevitable percentage of indulgers in *waipiro* we had not got the length of having thieves, for more than once I paddled down to the island, just tying up my tent-door and leaving everything to take care of itself; the danger of drunken intruders was left to be looked after by my nearest neighbour. But in giving you these extracts from my journal I have gone in advance of the day on which I intended to bring my personal memoirs to a close, and I must now once more take you back to the first four days of the year 1841 to chronicle the episode with which I shall wind up in the next, my last chapter.

CHAPTER XII

An Episode : Our First Maori Scare : Conclusion

IT was at a very early stage of the existence of the embryo capital, when we were all squatters, and the survey lines of the town were only half cut, and when we were all helping each other to do nothing until the first sale of town lots should come off, that we were turned aside from the even tenor of our do-nothing ways by the startling intelligence that the Maoris were going to drive us all into the sea, not to mention the possible, much worse fate of being killed on dry land, then eaten, and—O Sydney Smith! author of the saying—disagreeing with the Maori who had devoured us!

Early one morning the shadow of a stranger darkened my tent-door; he was not of the capital, for I knew every man, woman, and almost every child in the place.

'Here is a letter from Motu-Korea, sir; I have just come up from the island.'

The letter told me the bearer had a story to tell, and when told it amounted to this: A party of natives had called at the settlement where dwelt this messenger of evil tidings, then living in peaceful and happy vegetation with the Maori wife of his choice, or rather of the chief's selection for him, and who, on arrival of the visitors, had, of course, gone to smoke the accustomed pipe of gossip with them.

Part of the gossip was that a certain tribe had heard from some other tribe that a great massacre of all the

Pakehas had taken place at Kororareka, and that the per-petrators were in full march to sack the young capital, intending some fine morning to breakfast off the settlers and carry off the unconsumed remainder into captivity for future cannibal feasts. The particulars of the past mas-sacre and intended future proceedings had been given with such careful details that, of course, there could be no doubt of the thing. The very speeches of the different chiefs were repeated with the most faithful accuracy. Now, unless these speeches had been delivered, how could the very words be known? And so this Pakeha-Maori swallowed the whole tale as told him by his darker half, and having got the idea into his head it grew and magnified, and took such form and shape that in the darkness of the night the frightened couple took to a dinghy and pulled away for dear life to warn the authorities at the capital, and run the risk of, at all events, being eaten in good company.

He had arrived at Motu-Korea in the middle of the night, told his tale, and now he was passed on to me. I had to tell my visitor, even as he had been told at the island, that I believed the whole thing to be a cock-and-a-bull story, and the best thing for him to do was just to go away quietly home again. But he had been feeding so long upon the story, and it had taken such hold upon him, that nothing would do but he must unburthen him-self of the tale to the Deputy-Governor.

A couple of hours might have elapsed since my un-expected visitor had proceeded to warn the authorities of the impending danger when a visible excitement began to prevail in the settlement, and groups of people could be seen in earnest conversation collected here and there. I had previously noticed one of the Government work-men passing down in a great hurry to the Government store, and then he returned with the storekeeper to Exclusion Bay at an equally smart pace. Then the store-keeper returned with one of the Officials, in whose coun-tenance was plainly depicted a mysterious importance, 'for the settlers were not to be thrown into a state of alarm until the Government had determined what steps ought to be taken in such a serious emergency'. Presently this Official—he had been taking stock of the rusty 'brown-besses' in the store—hurried past again at a brisk pace.

Now even if I had known nothing about the story of alarm, and had seen this Official getting over the ground at such a pace, I should immediately have exclaimed, 'Hullo! what's up? what's happened?' for nothing in those days, except an innocent shower of rain, caused anyone to be in a hurry. There were no offices opened at certain fixed hours requiring punctual attendance; no counting-houses, no banks, no court-houses—except those 'under the canopy of heaven', and even these, by-the-bye, were still in the future—no anything requiring the presence of anyone at a given hour, except, perhaps, the workmen at the Government sawpits—no hurrying into town in the morning and bolting midday dinners—half-an-hour only allowed for same—all that, was far, far in the future, when children still unborn would not need to postpone their breakfast on rainy mornings until the weather cleared up, and if it didn't, get *no* breakfast at all, and only cold potatoes and a drink of water for dinner. So when I saw the Official whisk past I said to myself, 'Ah! the story begins to work'. And so it had, and it was very useless for the Official to wear that mysterious face, for he had told the whole story to the storekeeper when taking tally of the rusty muskets, and of course, having been told in the strictest confidence, that secured its immediate transmission from the storekeeper on the same conditions to the first person he encountered, and it went all through the settlement like wildfire.

And thus it came about that I saw the dreadful news being discussed by knots of my friends here and there. I had kept cautiously inside my tent, but I could see all round about by peeping through the folds of the canvas opening. I was waiting the return of my informant, but he did not make his appearance. The fact was the Officials had him in safe keeping until they had determined upon the course that was to be taken, and the bane and the antidote were to go forth together. But the indiscretion of the Official's 'in strictest confidence' had fairly got the start, and by the time the original bearer of the story was released from Exclusion Bay supervision, every soul in the place knew that the infant capital of their adoption was threatened with extinction, and themselves with death by the tomahawk, and something worse afterwards, in gratifying the alimentive peculiarities of their murderers.

My patience had at last become exhausted waiting for the return of my morning visitor, and seeing so much excitement prevailing outside, I was on the point of tying up my tent-door when the Deputy-Governor stepped in.

'Well,' said he in the cheeriest tone possible, 'what do *you* think of our Pakeha-Maori's story, eh? Serious, very!'

'Very,' replied I in the most serious tone I could assume. 'I almost feel as if I were half-digested already.'

This was too much for the Deputy, and drawing the tent-door together, he burst out laughing. I kept him company.

'I really would treat the whole story with ridicule,' he continued, 'but I am not alone, and my official colleagues, with whom I must consult, and who do not know the Maoris, consider that certain precautions ought to be taken, and I have had to waive my own opinion. The decision come to is that all hands are to be asked to turn out and keep a nightly patrol of pickets to skirt round the ridges of the different bays, and in case of anything suspicious being seen the alarm is to be given, when all are to fly and take refuge at the Barrack Point, and as it is a very defensible spot, we are there to make a stand for dear life', concluded the Deputy in a mock tone, looking woefully at me, when we both had a good laugh for the second time. Seeing that both he and I knew that the

one desire of the Maori at that epoch was to get the
Pakeha to come and live at their settlements, we might be
excused for being merry.

'The patrols will commence to-night, and meanwhile
we are sending to warn our few outsettlers into town,
and I have now come to offer you my gig and crew to
go to Motu-Korea to place it in the power of its solitary
occupant to join you here.'

Well, to the island I went, and reported the great
furbishing of muskets which had followed the telling of
the Pakeha-Maori's story, but as I could tell no more
news than that which had been first told last midnight
on the island itself, I was only the bearer of a message
back to the Deputy-Governor 'that if there was nothing
more to go upon than the original story, Motu-Korea was
just as safe a place to live in as the capital; that at the
former there would be no patrol work to break in upon
a comfortable night's rest; and that as to the island furnishing the wherewithal for any whetting of cannibal
appetites, that contingency was going to be risked without any fear, and many thanks to the Deputy-Governor.'

On my return to town I found that everything was in
full swing, and that I had been put on the first watch
of pickets to patrol along the ridge between Store and
Waipiro Bays, and our duty was to watch for the enemy
coming *down* the harbour to attack us. The other extreme
point was the lowest side of Mechanics' Bay, from
whence any enemy coming *up* the harbour could be seen.
From these two points a cordon of pickets would encircle
the entire settlement. Certain centres of communication
were fixed on where the sentries were to meet and report
and change guard. If anything in the shape of Maoris
appeared the sentinel was to fire off his musket as the
signal of alarm, when the women and children were to
hasten to Barrack Point, and all the male population capable of bearing arms were to muster at Exclusion Bay,
and then those who had not got firearms would be furnished with them—so far as such were forthcoming. The

patrols were all to fall back on the muster-place, where
the united army would be taken command of by the
Commander-in-Chief.

And thus it fell out that one morning we all arose
in blissful ignorance that before set of sun we should all
be in martial array with shouldered arms going our
rounds and swearing on our rusty muskets that we would
die the death, if necessary, in the defence of the wives
of our bosom, of the children of our loins, and of the
dear household gods of our tents and breakwind huts
against the attacks of all Maoris with cannibal thoughts
intent!

And so that night the infant capital's denizens retired
to get what slumber and rest they might, watched by the
faithful patrols, and the patrols paced their rounds,
bringing their reports to headquarters that 'all was well'.

And so the night passed and the sun rose smiling as
brightly as ever with his morning rays of salutation over
the waters of the Waitemata and the still-extant infant
capital.

We got no more news that day; some Maoris arrived
with their ordinary canoe-load supplies of pigs, potatoes,
pumpkins and maize for sale; but somehow, instead of
allaying suspicion, it only seemed to arouse it. Their coming was a mere blind to put us off our guard; they were
evidently constrained in their manner, and had not one of
them positively refused to sell a pig unless he could get
powder in exchange?—*that* spoke volumes.

So again that night the 'sentries paced their weary
rounds', only there was no weariness about it; it became
quite a pleasant interlude in our monotony, and we all
waxed exceedingly brave, and some were heard to say
they only wished the savages *would* come, 'and wouldn't
they catch it and get a warm welcome!'

In my patrol we had some very *choice spirits*—in
more acceptations of the term than one—and instead of
going home after the three hours' duty on guard, the
Store Bay headquarters found many collected there sing-

ing in grand chorus, 'We won't go home till morning'—
and, what is more, they didn't! What self-sacrifice thus to
watch over the innocent slumbers of their beloved in
their homes!

And again the sun rises, lighting up with his morning
rays the little white tents still peacefully imbedded
among the high fern.

But the time approached, and the night was at hand,
when these valiant spirits, who constituted the protection
of the infant capital now struggling into life, would be
put on their mettle when the dread cry 'The foe, they
come!—they come!' would break upon the stillness of
the night.

I had just returned to my tent after the first night's
watch, and had lain down on my fern bed, when there
rang on my ear the report of a musket from the very
point where I had just given over my sentinel duty on
the western cliff overlooking Store Bay, and from which
you could see up the harbour.

The signal of alarm was taken up, and I could hear it
sounding along the whole patrol line.

What! had I been mistaken?—the Maoris coming to
attack us? Impossible—won't believe it—a gun gone off
by accident, and the signal has been caught up through
this mistake.

I went forth. There, already, through the darkness, I
saw a rush being made to the place of rendezvous—not
that there were so many to make any great rush, but I
saw the dark figures going at the double-quick!

'The Maoris are coming!—the Maoris are coming!'
was the cry.

'Where?—where?' in vain asked I.

'Don't know—Maoris are coming!—Maoris are coming!—down the harbour,' came from a voice.

And on they rushed, women in haste, with dishevelled
hair and scant attire—luckily it was the height of summer—pressing to their bosoms their last-born, men with
older offspring in their arms, and lugging after them

older still, in hot haste through the darkness of the night to the Barrack Promontory.

I rushed down to the beach at Store Bay, but could see or hear nothing—'darkness there and nothing more' except myself, and I took that off away over the hill to Exclusion Bay. There I found the mustering of the forces and the serving out of the old 'brown-besses', and the colonial surgeon (an old army doctor) busy drilling an awkward squad, and then pop the guns began to go beside me.

'But the *Maoris*?' said I, 'where—which way are they coming?'

'Down the harbour—down the harbour; they will be in Store Bay by this time.'

And whisk went a ramrod past my ear!

'By Jove! Maoris would be safer than this', I said to myself. 'The sooner I'm off the better.' And off again I bolted, and made a rush back again to Store Bay.

There I found someone peering through the darkness.

'What have you seen?'

'Something slowly pulling round the point for Exclusion Bay.'

'The devil you have! You don't say so.' And away I rushed like a madman up the hill again to the other bay; and as I gained the height, and was speeding down the hill, I saw the brave advanced guard make a rush to the beach, and bang—bang—bang went a volley.

And then there came a terrible and fierce cry from the enemy from out the darkness of the waters.

'Hullo on shore there! What the devil are you up to, bang-banging away with bullets in your guns? Do you want to kill some of us?'

And a great huge mass came floating on to the shore.

It was a raft of timber from the Manukau ranges* brought down the harbour by a sawyer, with a native boat's crew, and it was the song of the Maoris which had caused the signal-gun to be fired!

[* Campbell presumably meant by this the *upper Waitemata* ranges.]

And thus it fell out that the infant capital was permitted still to wear its swaddling-clothes, and was not blotted out from off the face of this fair world and numbered amongst the things that were, but the sun continued to rise and smile upon her with his morning rays glancing along the sparkling waters of the Waitemata. Soon all that was remembered of the frightened Pakeha-Maori's story was the jollification of the patrollers who didn't go home till morning, and a little bit of spicy scandal against one frighted couple, who, having miscounted the number of their too numerous progeny, discovered in a corner of their *whare,* on getting home from the Barrack Point, one little pledge of love sweetly sleeping over the danger, the inno-cent's absence never having been missed!

Ah, how difficult to realize that the infant capital of that day has grown to its present proud position, and that the incidents I have narrated are facts of the past! Few now are those left who were actors in the scenes I have described; and in yet a little time none shall be left to tell the tale of the infant capital's early days and early ways, but to you this manuscript may draw the curtain aside and reveal past scenes to all others shut out for ever.

Many and trying were the vicissitudes we pilgrim fathers had to pass through. At first, during the great excitement of the first founding of Poenamo, co-existent with the adventitious prosperity of Australia, we all fondly believed we should make grand fortunes in three or four years. Yet within less than half that time not only this colony but Australia had reached the lowest depths of despair. When sheep were sold in that colony for nine-pence a head, and stations given in, you can well imagine what state we must have been in.

And then it was we were all put on our mettle, and had to prove of what quality it was. There are still one or two old friends who can well remember how I acted in my own person as master, clerk, and storeman.

And from no sordid motives did I fulfil these duties. The exigencies of the times we were passing through demanded every sacrifice.

We were struggling for very existence, there was no bright ray of hope, no silver lining to the dark cloud which overshadowed us, the future was a blank, and despondency was everywhere. Nearly every one of the young capital's first merchants came to grief and were blotted out.

I could turn up my journal and show you frequent entries of 'Working at the books and accounts until two o'clock in the morning—up again at seven.'

In such a crisis of one's fate, when it comes to the point of not making the two ends meet, is it right to keep clerks, and porters, and servants, and be grand, and trust to the future and a kind Providence to get one out of the mess? No, I never believed in that. Providence helps those who help themselves. No, when things come to that pass my motto is, 'Away with all false pride of station, put shoulder to the wheel, off coat, do the work, and fear not but your reward will come, for there is never degradation in honest labour.'

And my reward having come, it is needless to say I have no vain regrets in the past, and I look back with pride and pleasure to all I went through as a pioneer settler, and I have now the proud satisfaction of feeling that I fought the battle with a hard-working hand and a willing heart, and if the prize has been mine I have earned it.

Yes, take back again these my grey hairs, give me my last two score years to live over again, let me be one score and two years once more, and gladly would I again be the early settler of Poenamo.

But now that these grey hairs have come, I console myself in the belief that the pilgrim fathers who first dwelt at the infant capital did not live in vain. We who watched over its birth and first foundation, who stood by it during all its early struggles and through all its varying fortunes, did our part in developing the resources of the land of our adoption.

And we whom God has been pleased to spare are proud, in this year of grace, to compare the city of to-day with what it was in that long-ago past of which I have now told you so much; to have lived to see the great fern wilderness reclaimed; to have seen the infant settlement unrobe itself of its first primitive garments of brushwood, and of its breakwind fern huts and tents, and outliving its bush mask and wild appearance, enter on the path of progress.

And we have our reward that to-day we see that infant settlement grown into a city and proudly marching along the great broadway of civilization, and in all her young beauty growing up the slopes of her lovely shores—a city yet destined to be one of the fairest in the world, for what shores more beautiful than hers as they meet the glancing waters of her lake-like harbour? And from the crowning heights of these shores, what landscape more glorious than that which lies spread out in ever-varying beauty, stretching away in the far distance? To the eye it is a continual feast and joy for ever.

Proud am I to think on that shore I have made my home; content am I that on that shore, by the will of God, my own last long resting-place shall be.

APPENDIX

*To My Children**

I DO not sit down to pen these memoirs under the vain
delusion that the small events of my small life are
worthy of record.

But I think when I have passed away you ought not
to be in ignorance of your father's life, nor be placed in the
position of having to ask some stranger about those days
and myself when allusion is made to events of a long-ago
past in which it fell to my lot to act a somewhat prominent
part.

A simple narrative of my own writing seems to me the
most natural and fitting source from which you should
become acquainted with all I have passed through in the
early days of the first colonization of the country which
has become the land of my adoption and will be your own
future home.

To that far-distant land you are as yet strangers. Born
in the sunny clime of fair Italy, you have yet to learn that
there is a far-away land even more fair, with a still more
sunny sky, and a still more genial climate.

After many, many years spent in that land, and having
reaped the reward of my early struggles there, I am now
taking a long decade of holidays and wandering with you
o'er many lands, amongst the fairest cities and finest

[* This formed a postcript to the preface of the 1881 edition of
Poenamo.]

233

scenery of the old world, before we finally take our rest in our own home in the new world of the Great South Land.

I commence these my reminiscences, strange to say, in the 'land of the mountain and the flood', in my 'ain kintrie', whilst sitting on the banks of the Dee, the Braemar moorlands around me. In all likelihood, ere the last page is written I shall be once again in the far-away land where the scenes I am about to depict took place—scenes which can never occur there again, for civilization has replaced the reign of savagedom which prevailed in the days of the pioneer settlers.

And life then was of a primitive simplicity which can never be again, for now the iron road commences to span the land, and its very aborigines of the present day can no longer speak correctly their own language as spoken by their fathers two score years ago, so rapidly has that short epoch in the history of the colony changed all things.

I intend to divide these memoirs into two periods. The first period will refer almost entirely to myself and the native people amongst whom I was thrown after leaving the parental roof and starting for myself in the race of life. It will bring the period of it to the point when I changed the whole current of my life, making its stream thereafter flow in a new channel, when I joined the pioneer band who saw the birth and earliest years of the infant capital of a new colony born to the Crown of England.

The second period will deal more historically of the colony when my own individuality will have become merged in the increased population and advancement of the young settlement.

When I have brought my memoirs down to a date that you yourselves can take up the thread of my life and your own from your own memories—then I shall lay aside my pen.

It may be that you will not read what I intend to set down here until I shall have passed away and been gathered alongside of my brother pioneers, who have now almost all paid the last debt of Nature, leaving me in marked solitude, to be almost the only remaining link that binds the long-ago past with the present time, and who can tell you THE TALE OF THE EARLY DAYS OF POENAMO.

The following passages, also addressed to the author's children, were printed as a pendant to the final chapter of the book, after the entry, 'Conclusion of No. 1 Manuscript':

IT is even as I anticipated in my opening words to you, my dear children, and the conclusion of these my reminiscences has been penned in the land in which the scenes I have described took place.

Many years elapsed after closing the First Book before I again took up my pen to continue my narrative.

The banks of Deeside are now only to me a memory of the past. Never again shall I see her waters; never again on her banks shall a salmon rise to my rod; never again shall the grouse on her moors fall to my gun. The bracing moorland air of Braemar I shall never again inhale.

Memories of the past are they all—of a fatherland of long, long ago—memories which ever carry with them a halo of romance.

But a halo dimmed by the remembrances of the Romance and Reality of all that I have gone through in this land of my adoption.

I have told you only a 'plain unvarnished tale'; no word of fiction enters into it.

And if the perusal of this manuscript shall be to you a pleasure, to me, the writing it, has been a great solace, when repining at your absence.

All that is left me now to say is, 'What is writ is writ; would it were worthier!'

Index

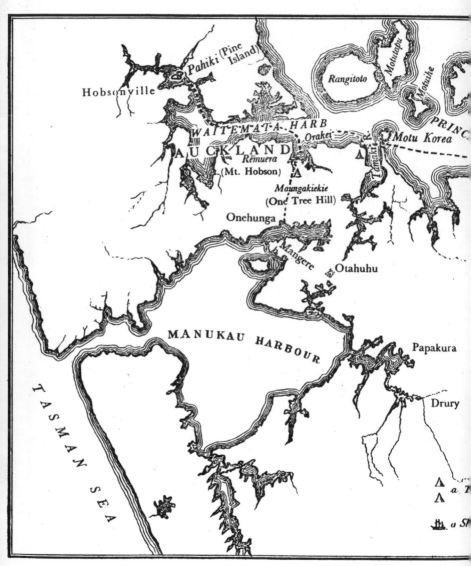

MAP OF THE DISTRICT D[
This map is an adaptation of